SPIRITUAL GIFTS

To my good friend Russ, I appreciate your balance and wisdom

Bobby

by
Dr. James Robert Clinton
Assistant Professor, Leadership Training
School of World Mission
Pasadena, California

Horizon House Publishers
Beaverlodge, Alberta, Canada

ISBN 0-88965-071-3

18,000 copies in print

Horizon Books
are published by Horizon House Publishers
Box 600, Beaverlodge, Alberta T0H0C0
Drawer AA, Cathedral City, CA 92234
Printed in Canada

TABLE OF CONTENTS

PREFACE TO THE REVISED EDITION--1983

This book was originally written while I was Director of the Learning Resource Center of the West Indies Mission (now called WORLDTEAM). I am grateful for the time and backing that the West Indies Mission gave to this project. The West Indies Mission also printed and distributed the original edition of Spiritual Gifts. Some 6,000 to 10,000 books have been sold. This has been gratifying for there has been little attempt at advertising. Basically, the book has sold via word of mouth recommendation. Now, however, I believe a wider market could profit from what I'm learning about spiritual gifts. This year the book has been translated into Chinese and is being published in Hong Kong for distribution among Chinese Christians. This revision, then, has several purposes: 1) to be appealing to a wider market and thus the need for a known publisher to market it; 2) to contain my latest understanding of spiritual gifts, for I have continued to learn over the 8 years since I first wrote Spiritual Gifts; 3) to include a new section which is designed to aid groups to study through the manual in an orderly way.

My own original study of spiritual gifts was triggered in 1967 by a set of tapes by the Rev. Bill Munnerlyn , now a pastor in Hacienda Heights, Ca. My special thanks go to Bill for his input into my life. His special help was in the Greek exegesis of the passages on spiritual gifts. This original study was reinforced at Columbia Bible College in a Philosophy of Missions course taught by J. Robertson McQuilkin. In a brief survey into spiritual gifts, Mr. McQuilkin gave underlying principles which I have come back to time and time again in my further detailed research into the topic. A research paper entitled, "My Spiritual Gift," in 1967 in conjunction with that class forced me to think through the whole process of identifying and setting forth a plan to develop and use my gift. I have followed through in the past 16 years on the plans set forth in that paper. I am indeed grateful to Mr. McQuilkin for his foundational teaching on this subject.

I taught spiritual gifts both in small group Bible studies off campus and in classes at the Jamaica Bible College where I was a missionary with the West Indies Mission. Those teaching experiences forced me to develop ideas about identification and development of gifts. Eventually I saw that what I was teaching should be put in a self-study format. For if I could reduce my teaching on spiritual gifts to a self-study format many more people could benefit and class room time could be used for interacting over student understanding of the concepts rather than lecturing on the concepts. That led to the writing of Spiritual Gifts in 1975. Perhaps that also explains the highly referential style of writing (a self-study technique called Information Mapping which identifies pieces of information for quick recall and identification).

I've learned several things in teaching spiritual gifts. A major lesson I've learned is how to emphasize gifts to people who have had little or no teaching on them. I've concluded that THE BIBLE EMPHASIZES THAT BELIEVERS SHOULD USE THEIR GIFTS. Whether or not they can identify or develop them is secondary. The study of gifts can easily sidetrack people to become overly occupied with identification of gifts. And often in churches with limited organization, believers don't use their gifts, and so can't easily identify them. This can be frustrating. It is in the context of service that gifts emerge. Therefore, I "tone down" my stress on identification and development of spiritual gifts at local church levels of leadership. The important thing is the proper functioning of the body and precise knowledge of one's gift is not necessary though most helpful.

I begin by introducing the concept of reciprocal living, rather than identification of spiritual gifts; that is, I stress the 75 or so "one-another" commands of Scripture. In order to obey them, believers will "naturally" use their gifts whether they realize it or not. Structure will emerge within the church not only to encourage reciprocal living but also to develop gifts in the context of service. Sue Harville's book, Reciprocal Living published by WORLDTEAM of Coral Gables, FL is a great resource for this emphasis. As interdependence develops, there is an openness to spiritual gifts. Teaching in this context does not frustrate. Believers can identify their gifts and use them more effectively.

I've learned lessons from Christians in other cultures. For many of them, this book is too theoretical and the use of tests and questionnaires is too Western. I've discovered that learning styles vary in different cultures. In the West, cognitive emphases are helpful, whereas many non-western cultures are more experientially oriented. I recommend that non-westerners use these identification aids with caution.

I don't understand everything about spiritual gifts. The Bible does not clearly answer all my questions. I've noted that some of my definitions are tentative and based on scarce biblical material. You may read other authors on spiritual gifts who are dogmatic about their definitions. I am not. I point out the biblical evidence as I see it and derive my definitions on that basis. I know I don't have the final word. Others help me see new material and see old material with new perspectives. Also, there are areas concerning spiritual gifts on which I have found no biblical data. I've noted these areas and indicated that principles or definitions are my own. Yes, there is still much to be learned.

One question that baffles me concerns the relationship between spiritual gifts and the fruit of the Spirit. My Christian heritage taught me that gifts are most effective when backed by a life manifesting the fruit of the Spirit. But there are the rare exceptions to that principle. My Leadership studies have shown that a few people have exercised spiritual gifts in a widespread public ministry with miraculous results, yet their personal lifestyles don't exhibit much fruit of the Spirit. God seems to bless their ministry with success even though they do not personally exhibit Christ-like maturity and integrity in their inner lives. I struggle with this paradox. Most of us would desire greater Christ-like maturity, but we can't let our sense of imperfection keep us from using our gifts. And so I praise God that he does use our gifts in spite of our lack of maturity. I trust that you, along with me, will seek to exercise gifts out of a heart of loving concern for others in the power of a Spirit-led lifestyle which bears more and more fruit.

Bobby Clinton, August 1984

HOW TO USE THIS BOOK

introduction   Although this book was originally written for individual study,
               it has also been used by classes in schools and churches. This
               revised edition, therefore, has added a new section intended to
               be a guide for studying <u>Spiritual Gifts</u> corporately over a 13
               week period.

               TWO MAJOR WAYS TO USE SPIRITUAL GIFTS

individual   You may study <u>Spiritual Gifts</u> as an individual or a group.
or   Sections I, II, and III adapt to either method. Section IV,
group   added for corporate study, includes a 13 week schedule.

individual   I recommend that you study the Sections in their natural order.
beginner   In Section I you may wish to choose only the more relevant
               subjects but Section II should be studied in detail. Modules 1
               and 2 contain the biblical material and definitions. These are
               foundational. Section III contains the application. It is
               designed to help you implement a plan to develop your gift(s).

individual   I recommend that you look at the index of maps for each Section
with some   to choose a subject. Subjects are concentrated and labeled for
background   easy reference. I want to stress the importance of Section II
               for definitions and Section III for application.

13 week   Section IV gives the schedule for a 13 week study of spiritual
group   gifts. Each lesson contains its own objectives and assignments.
sessions   These assignments include mini-case studies, and reading of
               pages in Section I, II, or III as appropriate. There are also
               activities which aim at affective and experiential learning
               goals. There are opportunities to see how well you've learned.
               You'll find that no one person has to teach the class, rather
               one person acts as a facilitator. If students do their study
               and assignments, the class can be a dynamic session with
               questions and discussions. Hopefully, this dialogue will enrich
               the lives of the whole group.

extra   If your group can meet more than 13 sessions I recommend the
sessions   added sessions be spent on the "Identification Exercises" and
               plans for development. These sections are profitable studied
               together provided that everyone studies and participates in the
               learning.

WRITING STYLE OF THIS BOOK

This book is designed for both initial and referential learning. A cue heading at the top of each page lists the major subject discussed on that page. Within a given page labels in the left margin of each page will cue you as to the material in the block of material to the right. At the conclusion of subject areas there are feedback exercises which test whether or not you've learned the information. The referential labels may help you quickly discover what you need to know without the necessity for reading each block of material. You are encouraged to go at your own pace.

Information is grouped in

- Blocks (several on a page, each dedicated to one major function), and in

- Maps (one or two pages dedicated to a major concept), and in

- Modules (series of maps relating to some common overarching topic), and finally in

- Sections (a series of modules under a major function of the book.

There are frequent summaries, charts, pre-views and over-views to integrate your overall study. There are detailed tables of contents within Sections and Modules. Objectives at the beginning of a Module and tests at the conclusion will aid you in learning. All of these features are intended to motivate and coordinate your study.

It's not easy to study spiritual gifts. It requires dedication, involvement, and time. But if you want to study and take advantage of this self-study book, I know you will profit greatly. Many have. And it can become a handy reference tool to help you help others. Enjoy yourself as you study this important subject!

OVERVIEW: SPIRITUAL GIFTS
---

introduction   The nature of the church demands that God's people understand
spiritual gifts since the church (from one perspective) is
people functioning interdependently according to their unique
Christ-given gifts and ministering one to the other in love.
Since this is so, we as God's people need to use our individual
Christ-given gifts. Recognition of gifts encourages use of
gifts. However, don't get hung up on identifying your gift.
Rather, use what you have—talent, ability, or gift. And
minister one to the other in love. Gifts will emerge in this
process.

---

sections   Four basic sections make up this booklet on spiritual gifts.

SECTION   I. GENERAL THOUGHTS ON SPIRITUAL GIFTS

SECTION   II. HOW TO IDENTIFY YOUR GIFT

SECTION III. THE FUTURE USE OF YOUR GIFT

SECTION   IV. GROUP STUDY GUIDE

---

goals   At the conclusion of your study on spiritual gifts

- you will be able to list basic spiritual gifts and define
  them in your own words.
- you will have tentatively identified at least one gift God
  has given you.
- you will have drawn up a tentative plan for developing your
  gift and listed some specific ways to use it.
- you will be able to help others identify their gifts.
- you will be concerned that God's people learn their
  spiritual gifts and use them to benefit one another.

---

advice to   This book uses a type of writing called Information Mapping.
the student   Unique features that allow for initial learning and for
reference learning are designed into this Information Mapping
technique. Basically, information is concentrated into units
called maps. A map deals specifically with the treatment of
one subject. It does so in terms of small information blocks
which are easily identified by labels. Feedback questions aid
you in assessing your progress. You should normally proceed
through the maps in the order they are presented. However, due
to the ease of referencing related concepts (at the bottom of
each page you will see the phrase, "related maps" which
indicates other information helpful in understanding the
present map), you may find yourself skipping about to these
related maps rather than following the normal order.

GENERAL THOUGHTS ON SPIRITUAL GIFTS

PREVIEW: SECTION I. GENERAL THOUGHTS ON SPIRITUAL GIFTS

introduction	Section I. discusses some basic ideas about spiritual gifts. Reasons for studying, problems arising, and perspectives to guide you are given. Principles of truth drawn from the 4 major passages (discussed later in more detail) are listed. A descriptive definition of a spiritual gift is synthesized from these principles. This definition emphasizes service to the body which results in multi-dimensional growth. Illustrations from the early church are seen in the light of this multi-dimensional growth. Finally, an overview procedure for identifying and using one's gift is suggested.

contents
Section I.

objectives	● From the four reasons given for studying Spiritual Gifts you will list the reason most applicable to you and explain in your own words why this is so.
	● From the problems described you will list the two which have concerned you in your Christian experience and explain in your own words how and why they have concerned you.
	● Given summarized statements of the list of problems and list of guidelines applying to these problems and given also a list of symptomatic statements reflecting problems as presently seen in Christianity, you should be able to match the symptomatic statements with both the problem and guideline most closely related to it.
	● Given a mixed list of characteristic statements or phrases which relate to either the gifts of the Spirit or fruit of the Spirit, you will be able to separate the list into the two categories by underlining those statements or phrases which characterize the Fruit of the Spirit.
	● Given a list of 4 of the 5 concepts involved in the definition of a spiritual gift, you will be able to give in your own words the missing concepts.

PREVIEW: SECTION I. GENERAL THOUGHTS ON SPIRITUAL GIFTS (cont.)

objectives
cont.

● Concerning the 5th concept of the definition of spiritual gift, you should be able to match the three aspects of multi-dimensional church growth (to which spiritual gifts contribute) with statements which reflect the three aspects of multi-dimensional growth.

advice to
the student

You should read carefully the objectives listed above. Then you may wish to turn to the feedback section before reading any of the maps. The questions on the feedback pages reflect the objectives. See how many questions you can already answer. Note those questions you can't answer. Then read the various maps with those questions in mind.

4 REASONS FOR KNOWING YOUR GIFT

introduction | What is this hubbub on spiritual gifts all about anyway? Hasn't the church gotten along fine for hundreds of years without all of this fuss? Isn't this some new gimmick to get more people involved and really participating in their churches? What are you changing now? Some would agree that we shouldn't do anything new or change anything. Well, relax, we're not suggesting anything new. However, we may well be suggesting some changes. We're looking at what has always existed in church life right from the beginning of local churches recorded in Acts. And we should change if we aren't what we should be. Below are listed some reasons why we should be informed on the Biblical doctrine of Spiritual Gifts.

why you should know your gift(s) | Though it is not absolutely necessary to identify your gift in order to use it, it is certainly advisable to do so. And no Christian who finds out that there is teaching on the gifts can under God ignore such teaching. Here are some reasons why you should try to determine your spiritual gift.

1. You are advised in Scripture to do so. In fact you are commanded to exercise it and may not do so if you don't know what it is.

2. If you know your own gift you can take steps to develop it.

3. If you know your gift you can set priorities so that your gift can be used productively.

4. You will be satisfied and not frustrated because you will know that you are contributing to the overall effort of the body in the way you were meant to be contributing.

historical significance | A quick survey of the major times of spiritual renewal in church history indicates that with each of these great movements there was a proliferation of small groups, and a high degree of participation of lay individuals utilizing their basic talents, abilities, or gifts. By recognizing and using our gifts we may see a great spiritual renewal in our day.

SOME PROBLEMS AND SOME PRINCIPLES WITH SPIRITUAL GIFTS

introduction	The study of Spiritual Gifts can be controversial.Two extremes should be avoided--neglect of the whole subject because of problems and disagreements, and overemphasis on spiritual gifts as a cure-all for the church. Listed below are some problems as well as principles to help us avoid both of these extremes.
4 problems	• disagreement--there's disagreement among evangelicals as to the definitions of the gifts and even the existence of certain gifts.
	• neglect--there's ignorance and even neglect of spiritual gifts in many churches.
	• confusion between supernatural and natural--there's confusion concerning the relationship between spiritual gifts and natural abilities.
	• abuse of gifts--certain spiritual gifts are emphasized by some as signs of a necessary work of the Holy Spirit. This emphasis at best causes spiritual pride and at worst can be divisive.
6 principles	
	• Disagreements usually indicate the lack of conclusive Biblical evidence upon which to resolve the question. Hence be tolerant and allow others their views without dogmatically insisting upon your particular view.
	• Begin slowly. Model the gifts. Teach without implying that what has gone on before is wrong. Recognize the ways gifts have already been used. Build on that.
	• Don't worry about distinction between gifts and natural abilities, but make sure you use both in service for God trusting him to use them to his glory. Ask him to clarify the distinctions if it will make your ministry more effective.
	•Beware of stressing one gift above another.
	• Encourage the exercise of gifts in the body but discourage using them as a sign of spirituality.
	• Make sure you know the difference between fruit of the Spirit and gifts of the Spirit. Fruit indicates spiritual maturity. Gifts are for service.
overall guidelines	• Remember that the teaching of spiritual gifts is fundamental to the concept of the church as an interdependent body. Although there are problems, it must not be ignored.

SOME PROBLEMS AND SOME PRINCIPLES WITH SPIRITUAL GIFTS (cont.)

- Trust the Holy Spirit to give whatever clarity is needed concerning gifts in order to make your group more functional as a New Testament church and bring glory to God through Jesus Christ.

related map see DISTINCTIONS BETWEEN GIFTS AND FRUIT OF SPIRIT, p. 18

DISTINCTIONS BETWEEN GIFTS AND FRUIT OF SPIRIT

introduction   The Scripture does not conflict with truth because all truth originates from God and will be consistent. However, from our standpoint there are apparent inconsistencies. Often the confusion lies with us and we need more understanding. Such is the case between the gifts of the Spirit and the fruit of the Spirit. The following chart will help clarify the differences.

CHART ON DISTINCTIONS

GIFTS OF SPIRIT

- Related primarily to the collective body of believers

- Related to ministry

- May be classified as to order of importance

- May be exercised in such a manner as to offend others, and cause discord and division in the body

- Normally no single believer receives all the gifts

- No gift can be demanded of all believers

FRUIT OF SPIRIT

- Related primarily to individual believers in body

- Related to character

- All are essential

- Can never be misused

- Every believer may bear all fruit all the time

- All of us can be commanded to manifest the fruit of the Spirit

Some
conclusions

- The Scriptural ideal seems to be the exercise of the gifts of the Spirit and the expression of the fruit of the Spirit concurrently.

- Both gifts and fruit are "signs" of the Holy Spirit in a life.

- Christ-like maturity is primarily indicated by manifesting the fruit of the Spirit, not by the presence of gifts nor even their powerful exercise.

Note: Basic chart ideas obtained from Prairie Overcomer article entitled, "Plumbline, Gift and Fruit Hand in Hand." Conclusions are my own.

FEEDBACK

1. Re-read the 4 reasons for studying spiritual gifts given on page 15.
    Although all 4 may apply to you generally one may apply more specifically
    at this present time.   Which reason most applies to you now?

    List the reason:

2. Explain how or why or in what connection you see this reason applying to
    you.

3. Read again the problems which arise concerning spiritual gifts. Probably
    you have been directly or indirectly involved in some aspect of one or
    more of the problems.   List the two problems that appear as most serious
    to you as you approach the study of spiritual gifts?

    Problem 1:

    Problem 2:

4. Explain in your own words why these problems are serious to you?

    Problem 1:

    Problem 2:

5. Check the statements below which relate to the Fruit of the Spirit.

    _____ a. related to character

    _____ b. related primarily to the collective body of believers

    _____ c. related to ministry or service

    _____ d. all are essential for any believer

    _____ e. can cause discord and division in the body

    _____ f. every believer normally expected to have

    _____ g. all cannot be demanded of every believer

FEEDBACK (cont.)

6. Given the following summarized statements of problems and guidelines, match the symptomatic problem statements listed below by placing the correct letters in the blanks.

<u>General</u> <u>Problems</u>

A. Disagreement on Definitions and Existence of for our day
B. Ignorance and neglect
C. Confusion between gifts and natural abilities
D. Emphasized as signs

<u>Guidelines</u>

a. Don't stress improper balance of some gifts to exclusion of some gifts.
b. Be tolerant and not dogmatic where Biblical evidence is not clear.
c. Use both for God's glory and allow him to bring out clarity needed in forming distinction between gifts and abilities.
d. Begin slowly. Model and teach gifts. Build on how gifts are presently being used.
e. Distinguish between exercise of gifts (allow) and using a gift as a sign of spirituality (discourage).

example

<u>De</u> (1) Everyone who wants all that God has to offer them should desire the baptism of the Spirit and hence speak in tongues.

_____ (2) Apostleship is not a gift but an office which was discontinued at the death of the eleven.

_____ (3) We expect it to be normative for each believer in our assembly to speak in tongues. To us this is the most important gift.

_____ (4) I don't believe that the gift of prophecy exists in the church.

_____ (5) Spiritual gifts cause more problems than they are worth. I think we should not allow any teaching about them in our church.

_____ (6) There are really only 7 basic gifts (see Romans list). All other "so called gifts" are merely ways of utilizing these 7 gifts.

_____ (7) Jane is such a good piano player. I believe God has given her the gift of piano playing in order to enhance our worship service.

_____ (8) Though we believe that all Christians have the Holy Spirit to some degree there is an evidence (tongues) of God's Holy spirit in a unique way which all should have who want maturity.

_____ (9) We pay our pastor to witness, preach, visit. Let him do the church work. That's what we pay him for.

_____(10) One who may be a good secular teacher may not be a good teacher since he was a good secular teacher <u>before</u> he was saved.

FEEDBACK (cont.)

Answers   Of course I can't give "right answers" for everyone for questions 1-
           4.   The questions are open-ended and require your choice.   (Really
           they just force you to think through these concepts for   yourself.)
           But I can give my answers which might be of help to some.

1. Reason which applies the most to me at this time:

    IF YOU KNOW YOUR GIFT YOU CAN SET PRIORITIES SO THAT YOUR GIFT CAN BE USED
    PRODUCTIVELY.

2. Wherever choices of service allow me to, I make decisions based on the use
    of my gifts of exhortation and teaching.   I try to take advantage of as
    many opportunities which use these gifts as I can.   On the other hand I
    usually turn down or at least minimize my scheduled involvements in
    activities which require other gifts to be in focus.

3. Problem 1 - NEGLECT: There is ignorance and even neglect of spiritual
                          gifts in many churches.

    Problem 2 - ABUSE: Certain spiritual gifts are emphasized by some   as
                            signs of a necessary work of the Holy Spirit.   This
                            emphasis at best causes spiritual pride and at worst
                            can be very divisive.

4. Problem 1 - NEGLECT: I am desirous of fellowship in a local church in
                          which I serve interdependently with others.   I want
                          to use my gifts to help them and in turn   I
                          desperately need the supportive ministry of   others.
                          I find that ignorance of gifts or neglect of them as
                          seen in the professional clergy/laity dichotomy that
                          exists makes it almost impossible to enjoy the body
                          life and ministry that should be.

    Problem 2 - ABUSE: Whenever I even begin to emphasize spiritual gifts I
                            am almost always faced with the "cautious ones" who
                            know of the "abuses" of spiritual gifts (tongues in
                            particular) and hence don't want to hear anything on
                            the matter.

5. _x_ a. _x_ d. _x_ f.

6. _De_ (1) _Ab_ (2) _Da_ (3) _Ab_ (4) _Bd_ (5)

    _Ab_ (6) _Cc_ (7) _De_ (8) _Bd_ (9) _Cc_ (10)

SOME BASIC IMPLICATIONS ABOUT SPIRITUAL GIFTS

introduction	The following statements are principles of truth drawn from the four major passages on spiritual gifts: I Corinthians 12,13,14; Romans 12:1-8; Ephesians 4:1-16; I Peter 4:7-11. You should certainly search out the Scriptures to insure that they are legitimately drawn from them.
basic principles of truth concerning spiritual gifts	• On the one hand spiritual gifts are sovereignly given by the Holy Spirit and yet on the other hand believers are admonished to desire the best gifts. • The Holy Spirit gives all the gifts necessary to accomplish his work in a local church. • Every believer has at least one gift. • A believer's gift may differ in degree and effectiveness and the way he exercises it from another believer having the same gift. • Each member with his gift is necessary to the whole body and therefore if any member is not active the body as a whole is weakened. • The gifts emphasize service to the body of Christ. • The motivation behind the exercise of a gift is love. • All of us as believers are to evaluate ourselves in terms of our God-given gifts. • We should recognize that our gifts will differ and hence we should have liberty to apply ourselves to the particular gift or gifts that are uniquely ours. • We should exercise our gifts in faith according to the depth of faith which God gives each of us. • How we exercise our gifts (that is, the motivating spirit behind the use of the gift and the attitude prevailing as we exercise the gift) is important as well as the fact that we do exercise it. • Each member should have an opportunity to use his gift interdependently with others. • People with leadership gifts are to train others so that every member will contribute to the overall growth of the whole body. • An awareness of the urgency of the times in which we live should cause us to give priority to exercising our gifts. • We will be held accountable for using our unique God-given gifts. • Gifts should be exercised authoritatively because of the assurance that we exercise them for God. • God should always receive the credit for our use of gifts whether they be leadership or supportive gifts. • The exercise of our gifts is a particularly Christ-centered way of bringing honor and recognition to God.
foundational	The previous statements and applications of statements form the basis for this unit on spiritual gifts.
related maps	see Summary of gifts passage — I Cor. 12-14, p. 38 see Summary of gifts passage — Rom. 12:1-8, p. 41 see Summary of gifts passage — Eph. 4:1-16, p. 42 see Summary of gifts passage — I Peter 4:7-11, P. 44

SPIRITUAL GIFT	synonym: gift(s), grace, measure of faith, manifestation of the Spirit

---

definition
A spiritual gift is
- a unique capacity
- given by the Holy Spirit
- given to each believer
- for service in connection with the church
- to cause the church to progress quantitatively, qualitatively, and organically.

---

examples of gift of exhortation in action

"Then when he had come and witnessed the grace of God, he rejoiced and began to encourage them all with resolute heart to remain true to the Lord" Acts 11:23.

"And after they had preached the gospel to that city, and had made many disciples, they returned to Lystra and to Iconium and to Antioch, strengthening the souls of the disciples, encouraging them to continue in the faith, and saying, Through many tribulations we must enter the kingdom of God" Acts 14:21-22.

---

example of teaching gift in action

"Now a certain Jew named Apollos, an Alexandrian by birth, an eloquent man, came to Ephesus; and he was mighty in the Scriptures. This man had been instructed in the way of the Lord; and being fervent in spirit, he was speaking and teaching accurately the things concerning Jesus, being acquainted only with the baptism of John; and he began to speak out boldly in the synagogue. But when Priscilla and Aquila heard him, they took him aside and explained to him the way of God more accurately" Acts 18:24-26.

---

example of gift of mercy in action

"Now there was in Joppa a certain disciple named Tabitha, which by interpretation is called Dorcas: this woman was full of good works and almsdeeds (mercy works) which she did" Acts 9:36.

---

comment
The above definition was synthesized from the basic principles of truth drawn from the four major passages of scripture on gifts. It seeks to go no further than that which is actually seen in the principles. Other things which would be nice to know about gifts aren't included in the definition because the Bible is actually silent on them. This definition does not answer some of the questions commonly posed by teachers of spiritual gifts -- when are spiritual gifts given? Where is the line drawn between natural abilities and spiritual gifts? Are all the gifts listed in Scripture? This definition is functionally descriptive. It seeks to provide an umbrella description under which the Biblically described gifts will fit to emphasize the central important idea of gifts rather than to clarify peripheral ideas which side track. In other words this definition seeks to major on the majors.

---

related maps
see 4 WAYS TO CATEGORIZE GIFTS, p. 46
see 3 KINDS OF GROWTH RELATED TO SPIRITUAL GIFTS, p. 25

HOW ONE RECEIVES SPIRITUAL GIFTS

introduction	The Scripture indicates that the bestowal of a spiritual gift is a sovereign act of the Holy Spirit (I Cor. 12:11). At the same time it indicates that believers (perhaps as a corporate body and not as individuals) can desire necessary gifts for ministry (I Cor. 12:31). How then do we receive spiritual gifts?

Some Possible Means of Receiving Spiritual Gifts

- by the laying on of hands (II Tim. 1:6),
- by the sovereign act of the Holy Spirit to confirm someone's words (Acts 19:6),
- coterminous with the reception of the Holy Spirit at the new birth (we know that each believer has the Holy Spirit from Rom. 8:9),
- coterminous with the Spirit's baptism of the believer into the body (I Cor. 12:13),
- by the Holy Spirit as needed on an occasion (such as a "Word of Knowledge" or "Word of Wisdom"; some would hold that these are not permanent gifts but are given situationally by the Holy Spirit),
- in answer to Spirit-led prayer for the necessary gifts as discerned by a group of believers in a given situation (I Cor. 12:31).
- by the principle of spiritual contagion. Some would interpret I Pet. 4:10 in this manner. That is, spiritual gifts may engender spiritual gifts. Many people within a group where certain gifts are being used may get those gifts. Of course other gifts will occur also.

comments	While we can not say for certain when or how the Holy Spirit does impart the gifts the above means are reasonable implications drawn from the Scriptures. We do know for certain that each believer has a gift (I Cor. 12:6ff). We are told to assess our gifts "according to the measure of faith" in Rom. 12:3. The implication in the context is that each believer does already have a gift and that it should be used according to the capacity for service inherent in the bestowal of the gift. In the major teaching passages on gifts it seems that all three passages assume people to already have a gift and further that some may have a gift without knowing it.
caution	In any case, whether seeking gifts or not, remember the admonition that better than all gifts is the heart motivated by love.

3 KINDS OF CHURCH GROWTH RELATED TO SPIRITUAL GIFTS

introduction   A spiritual gift was defined in terms of service a believer performs in order that the church progress quantitatively, qualitatively, and organically. Another way of saying "PROGRESS" is growth. Progression then is in terms of the 3 growths presented here.

definitions   <u>Quantitative church growth</u> refers to addition of people to the church through the initial phase of evangelization so that these people become responsible members of functioning local churches.

    <u>Qualitative church growth</u> refers to the process of individual and group maturation toward Christlikeness whereby members relate to God and one another as responsible members of a community which worships together, studies Biblical truth together, enables one another, and evidences concern for the spiritual vitality of each of its members toward Christ-like living.

    <u>Organic growth</u> refers to the process whereby the leadership of the local church emerges to provide the framework for a formal or informal structure which best unifies the corporate life of the local church and enables it to progress quantitatively and qualitatively.

KIND OF GROWTH	BASIC IDEA	PRIMARY THRUST	ABBREVIATION	SYMBOL
overall church growth	total progress in church growth	inward and outward	C G	
quantitative church growth	numerical expansion	outward – new people	N C G	
qualitative church growth	growth in maturity within the church	inward – own members	M C G	
organic	growth in orderly control and direction of corporate life	inward and outward	O C G	

3 KINDS OF CHURCH GROWTH RELATED TO SPIRITUAL GIFTS (cont.)

examples of quantitative growth	A recurring subject in Acts is the growth of the church. The following passages illustrate quantitative growth. Note emphasis of underlined words or phrases.

- Acts 2:41 "Then they that received his word were baptized: and there were added unto them in that day about 3000 souls."
- Acts 2:47 "And the Lord added to the church daily such as should be saved."
- Acts 4:4 "Howbeit many of them which heard the word believed; and the number of the men was about five thousand."
- Acts 9:31 "Then had the churches rest throughout all Judea and Galilee and Samaria, and were edified; and walking in the fear of the Lord, and in the comfort of the Holy Ghost, were multiplied."
- Acts 16:5 "And so were the churches established in the faith, and increased in number daily."
- Matthew 28:19 "Go ye therefore, and teach all nations, baptizing them in the name of the Father, and of the Son, and of the Holy Ghost."

examples of qualitative growth	Note emphasis of underlined words or phrases.

- Matthew 28:20 "Teaching them to observe all things whatsoever I have commanded you: and lo, I am with you alway, even unto the end of the world."
- Acts 2:42 "And they continued steadfastly in the apostles' doctrine and fellowship, and in breaking of bread, and in prayers."
- Acts 2:44 "And all that believed were together, and had all things common."
- Acts 2:46,47 "And day by day, continuing steadfastly with one accord in the temple and breaking bread at home they took their food with gladness and singleness of heart, praising God and having favor with all the people."
- Acts 4:32 "And the multitude of them that believed were of one heart and of one soul: neither said any of them that aught of the things which he possessed was his own; but they had all things common."
- Acts 5:42 "And daily in the temple, and in every house, they ceased not to teach and preach Jesus Christ."
- Acts 6:7 "And the Word of God increased; and the number of the disciples multiplied in Jerusalem greatly; and a great company of the priests were obedient to the faith."
- Acts 12:5 "...but prayer was made without ceasing of the church unto God for him."
- Acts 14:21,22 "And when they had preached the gospel to that city, and had taught many, they returned again to Lystra, and to Iconium, and Antioch, confirming the souls of the disciples and exhorting them to continue in the faith, and that we must through much tribulation enter into the kingdom of God."
- Acts 16:5 "So the churches were strengthened in the faith and increasing in numbers daily."

3 KINDS OF CHURCH GROWTH RELATED TO SPIRITUAL GIFTS (cont.)

examples of
qualitative
growth
cont.

- Acts 18:23 "And after he had spent some time there, he departed and went over all the country of Galatia and Phrygia in order strengthening all the disciples."
- Titus 2:1 "But speak thee the things which become sound doctrine: That...."(and follows many commands toward positive Christ-like living day by day).

---

examples
of
organic
growth

- Acts 6:2,3,4 "Then the twelve called the multitude of the disciples unto them, and said, It is not fitting that we should leave the word of God, and serve tables. Wherefore brethren, look ye out among you seven men of honest report, full of the Holy Ghost and wisdom, whom we may appoint over this business. But we will give ourselves continually to prayer, and to the ministry of the word."
- Acts 14:23 "And when they had appointed for them elders in every church, and had prayed with fasting, they commended them to the Lord, on whom they had believed."
- Acts 15:1-35 The entire passage illustrates organic growth functioning for the corporate good (this particular illustration of organic growth is taking place at regional church level rather than local).
- Acts 20:17,28 "And from Miletus he sent to Ephesus, and called to him the elders of the church...take heed unto yourselves, and to all the flock, in which the Holy Spirit hath made you bishops to feed the church of the Lord, which he purchased with his own blood."
- Pastoral Epistles—The books of I & II Timothy and Titus opt for development of leadership and orderly direction and growth for the corporate body.
- Titus 1:5 "For this cause, I left thee in Crete, that thou should set in order the things lacking and ordain elders in every city as I had appointed thee."

HOW TO INSURE THAT YOU WILL PROFIT FROM TEACHING ON SPIRITUAL GIFTS

introduction   If you are a Christian who takes his Bible seriously and wants to obey truth and you have studied the passages from which the teaching on spiritual gifts is drawn then surely you are asking, "How can I apply this teaching to my own life and situation?" The procedure listed below helps you get an overall view of what you can do to obey truth concerning spiritual gifts.

STEP	PROCEDURE	COMMENTS
1.	IDENTIFY YOUR GIFT	SECTION II of this unit deals with with this procedure in a detailed fashion
2.	SET OUT A SPECIFIC PLAN TO DEVELOP YOUR GIFT	SECTION III of this unit deals with this procedure in a detailed fashion
3.	CHOOSE YOUR SERVICE IN TERMS OF YOUR GIFT	SECTION III gives some hints concerning this procedure.
4.	USE YOUR GIFT	Nothing will profit you as much as Spirit led teaching through experience.

related maps see How to Identify Your Gifts, p. 33

FEEDBACK

1. Supply (in your words) the missing concept of the definition of spiritual gift.

   Definition: A spiritual gift is
   - o a unique capacity
   - o given by the Holy Spirit
   - o to each believer
   - o _____
   - o in order that the church may progress quantitatively, qualitatively, and organically.

2. Show that you understand the definitions of multi-dimensional church growth to which spiritual gifts contribute by placing the Roman numeral of the kind of church growth in the blank beside the statements below. Please note the focus of the statement might be indicated by <u>underlining.</u>

   I.   Qualitative Church Growth
   II. Quantitative (numerical) Church Growth
   III. Organic Church Growth

   _____ a. Refers to the <u>addition</u> of people to the church to become responsible members of a functioning local church.

   _____ b. Has a definition which focuses on leadership emerging and enabling corporate life to progress.

   _____ c. Has a definition which focuses on maturity of the individual believer and groups of believers.

   _____ d. Acts 19:19,20 "And not a few of them that practiced magical arts brought their books together and burned them in the sight of all, and they counted the price of them, and found it fifty thousand pieces of silver. So mightily <u>grew the word of the Lord and prevailed."</u>

   _____ e. Acts 18:9,10 "And the Lord said unto Paul in the night by a vision, Be not afraid, but speak and hold not thy peace; for I am with thee, and no man shall set on thee to harm thee: for I have <u>much</u> people in this city."

   _____ f. Acts 15:22 "Then it <u>seemed good to the apostles and the elders,</u> with <u>the whole church,</u> to choose men out of their company ...."

   _____ g.

   _____ h.

   _____ i.

   _____ j. Has as its basic thrust growth in maturity within the church.

FEEDBACK (cont.)

_____ k. Has as its basic thrust growth, orderly control and direction of corporate life.

_____ l. Has as its basic thrust numerical expansion.

answers

1. ● <u>for</u> <u>service</u> <u>in</u> <u>connection</u> <u>with</u> <u>the</u> <u>church.</u>

2. __II__ a.   __II__ g.

   __III__ b.   __III__ h.

   __I__ c.   __I__ i.

   __I__ d.   __I__ j.

   __II__ e.   __III__ k.

   __III__ f.   __II__ l.

HOW TO IDENTIFY
YOUR GIFT

PREVIEW: SECTION II. HOW TO IDENTIFY YOUR GIFT

---

introduction   Section I gave some overall considerations concerning spiritual gifts. It concluded by suggesting a fourfold procedure to insure that you will profit from teaching on spiritual gifts.

1. Identify your gift.
2. Set out a specific plan to develop your gift.
3. Choose your service in terms of your gift.
4. Use your gift.

This section deals with the first procedure by giving detailed practical advice for identifying your gift. Five modules of information help organize your thinking for identifying gifts.

---

contents   <u>Description</u>   <u>Page</u>
Section II

Module 1. Correlating the Gifts Passages 34
Module 2. Study of the Spiritual Gifts 49
Module 3. Analyzing Yourself Subjectively. 96
Module 4. Having Your Gift Confirmed by Others 106
Module 5. Confirming by Experience 112

For a detailed table of contents see each introduction to each module.

---

objectives   In general, when you have finished Section II, you will have tentatively identified one or more of your gifts and should be able to identify gifts in those around you. For more specific objectives see the introduction to each module.

---

advice   Module 1 contains a detailed checklist to discipline you to do what is necessary to identify your gift. Please make certain that you use this checklist as you study through Section II. Then after completing Section II, come back to this checklist and make certain that you have done every possible item.

MODULE 1.   CORRELATING THE GIFTS PASSAGES

introduction   The module compares the 4 passages on spiritual gifts.   It
gives basic information which is necessary to your
understanding of the individual definitions of each spiritual
gift.   It gives the specific purpose of each passage in terms
of the immediate or remote context of the book as a whole.   It
lists the gifts from each passage, gives a comparative listing
of the gifts, and categorizes the gifts.   It also gives a
checklist which will help you study the entire Section by
providing you with lists of things to do and places to check
off what you have done.

contents
Module 1

objectives   By the time you finish this module you should be able to,

   ● list the 4 passages on gifts in order of amount of
     information provided on gifts,
   ● state in your own words the purpose of each of the 4
     passages in terms of its contribution to the book in which
     it occurs,
   ● identify gifts by name which occur uniquely in each passage,
   ● identify gifts which occur in more than one passage,
   ● identify at least one unique principle of truth from each
     passage,
   ● write in your own words the two basic emphases concerning
     the use of gifts which occur in all 4 passages,

advice   Read the feedback questions on page 48. The questions there are
to the   sample questions based on the above objectives.   See how many
student   you can already answer.   Then read the maps in this module with
               the above objectives and sample questions in mind.   Read to
               fulfill these objectives and to answer the sample questions
               (and the other questions which could be constructed just like
               the sample questions).

CHECKLIST TO FOLLOW IN IDENTIFYING YOUR SPIRITUAL GIFTS

instructions
- Complete the studies of definitions, explanations, forms, surveys, questionnaires as given in the unit.
- As you complete the various items come back to this checklist and note your progress.
- Finally, when you complete the entire section, come back and make sure you have completed every item on the checklist.

I. IN MODULE 2 -- STUDY OF THE SPIRITUAL GIFTS I HAVE DONE:

Have done Gifts	Studied or formulated definition			Observed Scriptural Illustrations			Seen this gift in the life of a great Christian			Seen this gift in some person I am acquainted with		
	yes	no		yes	no	ref.	yes	no	Who?	yes	no	Who?
apostleship												
governments												
healing												
miracles												
teaching												
pastoring												
tongues												
inter. tongues												
evangelism												
exhortation												
prophecy												
knowledge												
wisdom												
helps												
faith												
mercy												
discernment												
giving												
ruling												

CHECKLIST TO FOLLOW IN IDENTIFYING YOUR SPIRITUAL GIFT (cont.)

II. IN MODULE 3 -- ANALYZING YOURSELF SUBJECTIVELY -- I HAVE DONE:

Method of Analysis	Yes	No	Plan to do so	Write Here Any Indications and Suggested Gifts which may Correlate with the Indications
Personality Test p. 99				
Inward Conviction Questionnaire p. 102				

III. IN MODULE 4 -- HAVING YOUR GIFT CONFIRMED BY OTHERS -- I HAVE DONE:

Interviewed the following gifted people using the form on page 109?

Yes	No	Person	Having Gift of	Who Suggests my Gift(s) May Be

Interviewed the following friends who know me well enough to suggest my gifts using the form on page 109.

Yes	No	Name of friend	Who Suggests My Gift(s) May Be

IV. IN MODULE 5 -- CONFIRMING BY EXPERIENCE -- I HAVE COMPLETED THE EXPERIENCE QUESTIONNAIRE on page 114.

Yes	No	Gift or gifts indicated as a result of my experience.

HOW TO IDENTIFY YOUR GIFT

introduction   Four basic principles are given below which will aid you in
                identifying your gift. Under each of these principles are
                given some practical suggestions or illustrations or examples
                which relate to the basic principle. Some of the practical
                suggestions involve testing. Some of these tests are available
                in this unit on spiritual gifts. Some of the suggestions
                require interaction with others. Some can be done in a
                relatively short time. Some are done over a period of time.
                You should do those suggestions that can be done immediately
                and should set up a plan for carrying out those suggestions
                which involve longer time periods to carry out. The basic
                principles should be followed (as far as is possible) in the
                order listed below.

STEP	PROCEDURE	PROCEDURAL FOLLOW-UP SUGGESTIONS
1.	STUDY THE GIFTS THOROUGHLY SO THAT YOU CAN RECOGNIZE THEM IN PEOPLE.	1. Do personal Bible studies on the gifts or at least review someone else's studies. 2. Observe Scriptural illustrations of gifted people. 3. Study the lives of great Christians seeking to identify gifts in them. 4. Seek to identify these gifts in Christians you know very well or are presently associated with in a ministry.
2.	ANALYZE YOURSELF FOR BACKGROUND INFORMATION.	1. Use personality test. 2. Use inward conviction questionnaire.
3.	SEEK CONFIRMATION OF YOUR GIFT FROM OTHERS.	1. Get those who have the gifts of wisdom, discernment, teaching, or knowledge to give their ideas on your gift. 2. Ask your friends who know you well to identify your gift. 3. Primarily ask the church of which you are a functioning part to identify your gift.
4.	SEEK TO LET EXPERIENCE BE A DETERMINING FACTOR IN BRINGING OUT YOUR GIFT	1. Your church will increasingly be aware of your gift(s) as you function interdependently in it. 2. You will be aware of fruit resulting from the exercising of your gift interdependently with others. 3. You will realize an increasing personal satisfaction in what you are doing. 4. You will occasionally find that forced situations in your church will demand a needed gift which God may cause you to seek. 5. You will recognize especially in the leadership gifts that gifted people will attract like-gifted people.

SUMMARY OF GIFTS PASSAGE -- I CORINTHIANS 12 - 14

introduction	Though none of the four major passages on gifts has as its primary purpose an exhaustive treatment of the doctrine of spiritual gifts, I Corinthians 12 - 14 probably contributes the most information about spiritual gifts. However, we must be cautioned that when studying each of the major passages, one must first recognize the major purposes of the passage and interpret whatever teachings are given in the light of the purpose.
purpose of I Cor. 12-14 related to the book as a whole	Paul, in I Corinthians is dealing with a series of problems which confronted the church in Corinth. The letter as a whole has as its main purpose the solutions of these problems. The book as a whole teaches that church problems, individual or corporate, can be solved by submitting to God's revealed truth concerning those problems. To the various problems Paul does not just give an authoritative command or an arbitrary rule. He states the principles with which the problems are concerned and thus gives solutions which have value for us today. For while specific conditions today may differ from those of the Corinthian church, the problems dealt with are analogous and Paul's principles can often be reapplied to our situation. The problems to which Paul addresses himself are grouped as follows: an ecclesiastical problem—divisions in the church; then three moral questions—about discipline, law suits, impurity in social life; two questions of expediency—marriage, meats; three problems of public worship—conduct of women, practice of Lord's supper, and orderly exercise of spiritual gifts; and a final doctrinal problem— the resurrection. The purpose of I Corinthians 12-14 is aimed at the third and probably most important problem of public worship—the orderly exercise of spiritual gifts.
specific problem defined	Certain spiritual gifts (tongues singled out especially) were being regarded almost as ends in themselves rather than means used by God for purposes relating to his church. The use of these gifts for pride and gratification of the user was evident. Further, the particular gift singled out (tongues) was most highly prized though not the most useful by far. The exercise of these gifts was resulting in envy, spiritual pride, and divisions. Further, public worship services were being disrupted and were not accomplishing their God-given purposes because of the emphasis on exercising the gifts.

SUMMARY OF GIFTS PASSAGE -- I CORINTHIANS 12 - 14 (cont.)

Paul's basic answer to the problem	Paul answers the problems above by showing in

I Corinthians 12:1-11
- That the test of true spirituality involves submission to the Lordship of Christ.
- That all gifts are important because they come as a direct result of the Holy Spirit's sovereign ministry.

I Corinthians 12:12-27
- That all gifts are important because of the interdependent nature of the church.
- That the gifts operating harmoniously together, each contributing its function, should have as its purpose the edification of the church as a whole.

I Corinthians 12:28-31
- That the possession of no single gift is a test of one's spiritual maturity. Not all church members can be expected to have any one particular gift.
- That God has in fact given an order to the gifts which places what are sometimes called leadership gifts at the forefront and that the particular gifts being prized by the Corinthian church were quite far down the ladder. But even so, Paul's tone indicated that due to the interdependent nature of all gifts there should be no spiritual pride associated with any of these gifts.
- That, if there is a prizing of gifts, at least seek that which is most useful and beneficial to the whole church.

I Corinthians 13
- That a proper attitude behind our exercising our gifts, that of love, is essentially more important than the gifts or results of exercising those gifts.
- That love is an enduring quality while gifts are to be used in time.

I Corinthians 14
- That the relative value of spiritual gifts is to be tested by their usefulness to the church as a whole (contrast of prophecy and tongues is the example illustrating this).
- That joint participation of each gift in public worship should be in terms of edifying the whole church.
- That orderliness in public worship is consistent with the way God does things.

---

caution in drawing out teaching	Having recognized what Paul is trying to do in this passage it is well that we give some cautions in drawing out teaching on spiritual gifts. Paul does not purpose to give an exhaustive list of gifts nor to define the various gifts. He does not tell exactly how the gifts are to be used except to show that they are necessary because of the interdependent nature of the gifts. He does say the gifts should be used to edify and hence there should be an orderly and not confusing use of these gifts in public. He does show that love should be an essential part of our use of our gifts. Keep these limiting factors in mind, then, in observing the list of gifts and implications on these gifts.

SUMMARY OF GIFTS PASSAGE -- I CORINTHIANS 12 - 14 (cont.)

list of gifts	In giving the list it should be recognized that Paul names some gifts in verses 8-10 and gives another listing in verse 28. In verse 28 Paul names 5 gifts directly and indicates by metonymy in an indirect manner 3 other gifts by naming the people who exercise those gifts (apostles, prophets, teachers).

English translation

- apostleship

- prophecy

- teaching

- word of wisdom

- word of knowledge

- faith

- miracles (power)

- gifts of healings

- discerning of spirits

- kinds of tongues

- interpretation of tongues

- helps

- governments

principles	• On the one hand spiritual gifts are sovereignly given by the Holy Spirit and yet on the other hand believers are admonished to desire the best gifts.
	• The Holy Spirit gives all the gifts necessary to accomplish His work in a local church.
	• Every believer has at least one gift and may have more and may seek in God's will for more.
	• A believer's gift may differ in degree and effectiveness from another believer having the same gift.
	• Each member with his gift is necessary to the whole body and therefore if any member is not active the body as a whole is weakened.
	• The gifts emphasize service to the body of Christ.
	• The motivation behind the exercise of a gift is love.

SUMMARY OF GIFTS PASSAGE -- ROMANS 12:1-8

introduction	Though none of the four major passages on gifts has as its primary purpose an exhaustive treatment of the doctrine of spiritual gifts each contributes in some way to the information on gifts. Romans 12:1-8 does so by adding several new gifts to the list of gifts and by correlating the use of gifts with determining the will of God for our lives.
purpose of Romans 12:1-8 related to the book as a whole	Romans teaches that God's gracious provision of Christ's righteousness (= the Gospel of God) to every believer encompasses mankind's total need, is consistent with redemptive history, and applies to all of life's relationships. The passage touching on gifts occurs in the large section (12-15) which deals with the application of the Gospel to relationships of life—one of the practical outflows of the gospel is service to God. Romans 12 connects service to God and practical everyday living of Christianity back to what God has done in the Gospel. Romans 12:1-8 shows that true dedication to God involves ● surrender to him, ● a constant changing of our lives in spiritual maturity, ● a search of God's will which involves service for him in terms of a proper evaluation of one's gifts and exercising of those gifts interdependently with others.
list of gifts given	English translation ● prophecy ● ministry ● teaching ● exhortation ● giving (sharing) ● ruling (leading) ● mercy
principles	● All of us as believers are to evaluate ourselves in terms of our God-given gifts (12:3). ● We should recognize that our gifts will differ and hence we should have liberty to apply ourselves to the particular gift or gifts that are uniquely ours (12:6). ● We should exercise our gifts in faith according to the depth of faith which God gives each of us (12:6). ● How we exercise our gifts, that is, the motivating spirit behind the use of the gift and the attitude prevailing as we exercise the gift, is as important as the fact that we do exercise it. (Note the qualifying phrases—according to the measure of faith, sharing in simplicity, ruling diligently, showing mercy cheerfully.) ● Each member should have an opportunity to use his gifts interdependently with others (12:4-6).

SUMMARY OF GIFTS PASSAGE -- EPHESIANS 4:1-16

introduction	Ephesians 4:1-16, another of the major passages on gifts, contributes less to the actual information on gifts than does I Cor. 12-14 and Romans 12:1-8. However it is extremely important in that it connects the teaching of gifts to the eternal purpose of God for the church and thus implying that gifts within the church are an essential part of the nature of the church.
purpose of Eph. 4:1-16 to the book as a whole	Ephesians is primarily a book dealing with the church. It teaches us that the revealed wonder of the church demands a holy walk. The revealed wonder of the church relates to a cosmic purpose that God has for the church—to show his power and his ability to integrate into oneness diverse elements in the universe. This wonder of the church was revealed to Paul. Because of its wonder and eternal significance there are demands made upon believers to live out their part of this revealed wonder. The very first demand made upon believers to live out their part of this revealed wonder involves unity (Eph. 4:1-16). It is in this section of practical application toward unity that the Ephesian passage on gifts is given. Its primary purpose is to show that gifted leadership was given to the church in order that it might progress toward a unified spiritual maturity. It also indicates how these "leadership" gifts are part of an interdependent exercise of gifts of all members of the church. The proper interdependent exercise of leadership gifts and other gifts will bring about a maturity of oneness in believers and continued progress toward Christ-like living.
list of gifts	Again Paul indicates several gifts indirectly by metonymy naming the leaders rather than by directly naming the gifts. He does this to emphasize the important role the leadership gifts play in directing the church to maturity.

- apostleship
- prophecy
- evangelism
- pastor-teachers

note	The gift of evangelism which did not occur in Romans 12 or I Corinthians 12 is included in this list. By adding it to the apostles, prophets, etc., it would seem to rank in importance with them. The teaching gift is qualified here by the idea of shepherding (or vice versa). Some would list a gift—the pastoral gift—as a result of the inclusion of the pastor in this list of leadership gifts. Romans 12 lists a leadership gift in the concept of "ruling well." This could be a separate gift (perhaps different from I Cor 12 governments) and perhaps different from the above gifts. However, it may well be a quality describing how governments or the above gifts should be exercised. It is not clear from the context alone.

SUMMARY OF GIFTS PASSAGE -- EPHESIANS 4:1-16 (cont.)

---

principles
of truth
drawn
from
Eph. 4:1-6

- People with leadership gifts are to train others so that every member will contribute to the overall growth of the whole body.
- The church as a whole will **not** reach a unified maturity unless each of its members is exercising his gift in concern with other members.

---

possible
differences
of inter-
pretation

- Some would not interpret the list given in verse 11 as representing (by figure of speech -- metonymy) gifts **but leaders given to the church**. However two of these "roles" are listed in parallel passages as gifts (prophecy, teaching). It seems logical to assume that the other two (apostles, evangelist) also represent gifts exercised by the men called by those names. As a matter of fact all gifts given to the church are in the form of people.
- Some would say that the leadership gifts listed here belong to the universal church (roving apostolic type ministry) and would thus say that the "saints" they are equipping would have "lesser" gifts. However, again other gifts passages describing local church situations mix these so-called leadership gifts in with the "lesser" gifts and assume all of them present among the local saints.
- The King James phraseology, some pastors and teachers, has been interpreted in various ways. Some would say they represent two distinct people. If so then to be consistent and interpret by metonymy one would have to have a gift of pastoring as a distinct gift apart from the teaching gift. Others interpret the original Greek construction **not** as pastors and teachers **but** as pastors who also are teachers. Again to be consistent in interpreting by metonymy this is a gift of pastoring which includes with it the gift of teaching.

SUMMARY OF GIFTS PASSAGE -- I PETER 4:7-11

introduction	The passage in I Peter 4:7-11 is one of the four major passages which mention spiritual gifts. Being a brief passage it gives less information concerning spiritual gifts than the other three passages.
purpose of I Pet 4:7-11 in terms of the book as a whole	I Peter teaches that God is in control of everyday circumstances and is using them to perfect our trust in God. Because this is true Peter demands that believers must submit to God's purposes in circumstances around them in governmental regulations, in societal relationships, in marital relationships, in relationships with Christian brothers. The particular passage touching on gifts is exhorting Christian brothers in their relationships. It particularly is emphasizing the kinds of practical signs which should be seen as a result of a believer's expectancy of the second coming. The signs include: • a sincere expectant prayerful attitude, • a love among brothers in Christ which overlooks their faults, • exercising hospitality one to the other, • an exercise of one's God-given gifts.

gifts indicated	Peter does not seem to list any gifts by name but indicates the basic method whereby several gifts could be exercised.
	
	      • speak
	      • minister

hospitality	Some would see a gift of hospitality in this context since Peter does mention a command for believers to use hospitality with one another. I prefer to interpret this command as one of the many reciprocal living commands that all believers are required to do and not a listing of a gift. It is a general command just as "speak" and "minister" are general commands.
principles of truth from I Peter 4:7-11	• An awareness of the urgency of the times in which we live should cause us to give priority to exercising our gifts (I Peter 4:11). • We will be held accountable (as good stewards of the manifold grace) for using our gifts (I Peter 4:10). • Gifts should be exercised authoritatively because of the assurance that we exercise them as from God (I Peter 4:11). • The exercise of our gifts is a particularly Christ-centered way of bringing honor and recognition to God (I Peter 4:11). • God should always receive the credit for our use of gifts whether they be leadership or supportive gifts (I Peter 4:11).

COMPARATIVE LISTING OF GIFTS FROM 4 PASSAGES

COMPARATIVE LISTING OF GIFTS			
I Corinthians	Romans most likely the same as	Ephesians most likely the same as	I Peter most likely the same as
apostleship		apostles	
prophecy	prophecy	prophets	speaketh ?
teaching	teaching	pastor-teacher	speaketh ?
word of wisdom	exhortation ?		speaketh ?
word of knowledge	exhortation ?		speaketh ?
faith			
miracles (power)			
gifts of healing			
discerning of spirits			
kinds of tongues			
interpretation of tongues			
helps			
governments	ministering ruleth?	pastor-teacher	ministering
		evangelists	
	giving		
	mercy		
	ruleth		

THINGS COMMON TO ALL PASSAGES (OCCURS IN DIRECT CONTEXT OR IMMEDIATE CONTEXT).

1. A stress on love motivating the actions of believers.

2. The idea that gifts are used to minister to one another.

3 WAYS TO CATEGORIZE GIFTS

I. In terms of interdependent functioning resulting in church growth.

GIFTS HAVING A PRIMARY FOCUS TOWARD

Maturity Church Growth		Numerical Church Growth	Organic Church Growth
prophecy knowledge exhortation tongues discernment interpretation of tongues	teaching wisdom faith giving pastoring	apostleship evangelism miracles healing mercy	governments helps ruling

II. In terms of how best exercised.

BEST EXERCISED IN TERMS OF

Gathered Church	Dispersed Church		Both	Regional
	to unbelievers	to believers		
prophecy knowledge wisdom governments	tongues interpretation of tongues mercy evangelism	helps faith discernment giving evangelism	teaching pastoring wisdom knowledge exhortation apostleship evangelism	apostleship evangelism miracles healing

III. In terms of leadership/supportive roles.

LEADERSHIP GIFTS	SUPPORTIVE GIFTS		
apostleship teaching pastoring evangelism prophecy ruling	healing miracles helps faith tongues	mercy discernment giving wisdom interpretation of tongues	exhortation governments knowledge

HOW GIFTS AND KINDS OF GROWTH ARE INTERRELATED

introduction   The three kinds of growth interrelate to one another.   Certain
kinds of gifts apply more directly to one kind of growth than
another. These relationships are seen in the diagram below.

PROCESS SHOWING GROWTH RELATIONSHIPS

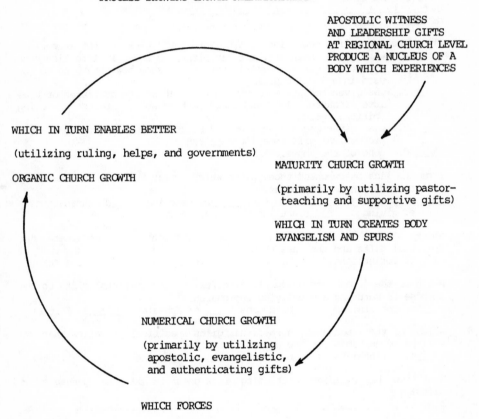

APOSTOLIC WITNESS
AND LEADERSHIP GIFTS
AT REGIONAL CHURCH LEVEL
PRODUCE A NUCLEUS OF A
BODY WHICH EXPERIENCES

WHICH IN TURN ENABLES BETTER

(utilizing ruling, helps, and governments)

ORGANIC CHURCH GROWTH

MATURITY CHURCH GROWTH

(primarily by utilizing pastor-
teaching and supportive gifts)

WHICH IN TURN CREATES BODY
EVANGELISM AND SPURS

NUMERICAL CHURCH GROWTH

(primarily by utilizing
apostolic, evangelistic,
and authenticating gifts)

WHICH FORCES

related maps   see 3 Kinds of Growth Related to gifts p. 25 , 4 Ways to
Categorize Gifts, p. 46.

FEEDBACK ON CORRELATING THE GIFTS PASSAGES

Questions

1. List here the four passages on spiritual gifts in order of most information given about gifts.
    a. _____
    b. _____
    c. _____
    d. _____

2. The passage on gifts occurring in I Corinthians (check correct answer)
    _____ a. was given because the Corinthians had asked Paul to list the spiritual gifts, explain them, and show how they were to be used in a local church.
    _____ b. was given because Paul wanted to teach on the qualities of true love (chapter 13) and could best do so in terms of using spiritual gifts.
    _____ c. was given because Paul wanted to stress the importance of the prophetical gift to a local church.
    _____ d. none of the above.

3. From the list below check those gifts which appear uniquely (not named by that name elsewhere) in Romans.
    _____a. prophecy _____b. ministry _____c. teaching _____d.exhortation
    _____e. giving _____f. ruling _____g. mercy

4. Which of the 4 passages on spiritual gifts tell us to evaluate our spiritual gifts and then use them.
    _____a. Corinthians _____b. Romans _____c. Ephesians _____d. I Peter

5. Which of the 4 passages on spiritual gifts relates spiritual gifts to the purpose of maturing and unifying the church.
    _____a. Corinthians _____b. Romans _____c. Ephesians _____d. I Peter

6. Which of the 4 passages on spiritual gifts specifically implies that we will be accountable for how we use our gifts.
    _____a. Corinthians _____b. Romans _____c. Ephesians _____d. I Peter

7. What two basic ideas about using gifts occur in all the passages on gifts?
    a. _____

    b. _____

Answers

1. a. I Cor. 12-14 b. Romans 12:1-8 c. Ephesians 4:1-16 d. I Peter 4:7-11
2. __x__ d. It was given to correct the abuse of gifts—particularly tongues and to combat spiritual pride associated with certain gifts.
3. _x_d. exhortation, _x_e. giving, _x_f. ruling _x_g. mercy
4. _b_ 5. _c_ 6. _d_
7. a. A stress on love motivating the actions of believers.
    b. The idea that gifts are used to minister to one another.

MODULE 2. STUDY OF THE SPIRITUAL GIFTS

introduction   A first step in identifying your gift is knowing the definitions of the gifts given in Scripture. The ideal situation is to do original studies on each of the gifts yourself. If you can't do in-depth studies yourself then at least study my in-depth studies presented in this module. But don't take my studies for granted; remember, you should "search the Scriptures daily whether these things be so." Examine what I have done in the light of the Scriptures. Don't forget to go back to the checklist on page 35 and mark off each gift after you study it.

objectives   By the time you finish Module 2, you should be able to,
for
module 2   ● match names of gifts with kinds of growth,
    ● match the name of a gift with its definition,
    ● match a gift with its symptoms,
    ● match a gift with its primary uses,
    ● match a gift with a contextual description of it,
    ● match a gift with a Scriptural passage related to it.

advice   Read the feedback questions first. Then read through the various
to the   maps with these kind of questions in mind. Remember the feedback
student   questions are sample questions. More just like them could be constructed.

OVERALL PROCEDURE FOR ARRIVING AT DEFINITIONS OF SPIRITUAL GIFTS

introduction   Nowhere in the New Testament are the spiritual gifts defined
explicitly. Qualifying phrases help describe them. Some are
illustrated. Some of the functions that they seemingly involve
are commanded in the Scripture of believers (see particularly
the reciprocal commands). Thus any definitions of spiritual
gifts require interpretation. On some of the named gifts very
little else than word studies can be used to try to identify
them. Where this is the case one cannot be as dogmatic as one
would like. One can trust that God has providentially ordered
it so that where clarity or identity of a gift is needed for the
good of the ongoing of the church, God will have given it. There
is disagreement on whether or not all the gifts mentioned in
Scripture are extant today. It is the opinion of this author
that there are no exegetical arguments which exclude the
existence of any of the gifts today. One's system of
interpretation (or philosophy of closure with regard to
unresolved topics) may require such a position. However, one
can rest upon this—since the gifts are an essential part of the
interdependent nature of the church, the functions they
represent will be accomplished as God sees them necessary to the
ongoing of the church whether by the gifts named in Scriptures
or through other abilities, talents, etc. Where there is
disagreement on the existence of a gift for our day or where
there is some lack of clarity such will be mentioned.

basic   The following procedure was used to arrive at the definitions
procedure   of the spiritual gifts.

1.   A comparative study of the listing of the gifts resulted in a
      list of 18 gifts to be studied for a definition.

2.   The original words for the various gifts were studied
      contextually throughout the New Testament where such context
      implied some relationship to the gift under study.

3.   Study of passages where the use of the gift (or related
      function associated with the gift) were commanded were next
      analyzed to bring out the use of the gift.

4.   Finally, illustrations referring to the use of the gifts
      occurring in historical passages or non-didactic passages were
      studied. These passages primarily give precedence to the
      existence of the gifts and in some cases the function of the
      gift.

order   The gifts are presented in terms of their focus toward church growth.
of
presen-   MATURITY CHURCH GROWTH (11 gifts)
tation   NUMERICAL CHURCH GROWTH (5 gifts)
                   ORGANIC CHURCH GROWTH (2 gifts)

GIFTS FOCUSED ON MATURITY CHURCH GROWTH

introduction The following 11 gifts have as their primary focus either edification of or other ministry to the believers.

11 gifts
with
inward
focus

LIST OF MATURITY CHURCH GROWTH GIFTS

Gifts	Ministry in Connection With	
	Use of Revealed truth	Other
Prophecy	x	
Teaching	x	
Word of Knowledge	x	
Word of Wisdom	x	
Exhortation	x	
Tongues	x	
Interpretation of Tongues	x	
Discernment	x	
Faith		x
Giving		x
Pastoring		x

PROPHECY

introduction   A fair amount of information concerning the gift of prophecy occurs in the New Testament. In the early church there was no finalized form of the New Testament such as exists today for our use. God used the gift of prophecy to reveal truth to his people. The truth was predictive sometimes or simply new truth needed for the church. The truth was validated by those having discernment gifts. Both of the elements of predictive prophecy and forth-telling or expounding of truth appear in the New Testament as aspects of this gift. With the completion of the New Testament writings many feel that the need for new revelational truth ceased to exist. People holding this view will say that the gift no longer exists or exists only in terms of its forth-telling aspects. Some holding this latter view would say that the forth-telling function has been transferred to the function of the teacher. This gift ranked very high in the order of the gifts listed in I Cor. 10:27 (second only to the apostolic gift) and hence was certainly an important gift in the New Testament church.

Greek word (transliteration)	Etymological or literal rendering	Basic idea(s)	contextual Verification
<u>verb</u>	to show or make known before hand	to reveal future happenings which God has revealed	Acts 21:9-11 Acts 11:27-30 Rom 15:26
propheteuo		to publicly expound the truth of God in order to exhort or edify or comfort	Titus 1:12 I Cor. 14:3,4 Acts 15:32
<u>noun</u> prophetes		one who functions as a prophet	I Cor. 14:1,3,4,5
<u>noun</u> prophetia		that which is given by the prophet: name of the gift	I Thess. 5:20 I Tim. 1:18 Rom 12:6

definition   The <u>gift</u> <u>of</u> <u>prophecy</u> is the capacity to express truth (of a predictive nature as well as explanatory) from God in order to exhort, edify, or console believers and to convince non-believers of God's truth.

comment   A prophet is one who is deeply impressed that God has by the Spirit of God given him a message which he proclaims with authority and conviction. This message may result in further insight in God's Word, conviction of sin, reproof or comfort or a new direction that the church may take. Many times the message may speak to a prominent issue.

PROPHECY (cont.)

comment cont.	The prophet is not one who exposes the Word but one who exposes God's will. The gift may be limited to a local church or broadly used beyond local churches.
example	Acts 15:32 "And Judas and Silas being prophets also themselves exhorted the brethren with many words and confirmed them."
comment	This gift seems to have been exercised in the gathered church.
Scriptural function of the gift's forth-telling aspect	I Cor. 14:3 "But he that prophesieth speaketh unto men to edification and exhortation and comfort."
effect of the gift on unbelievers	I Cor. 14:24,25 "But if all prophesy and there come in one that believeth not, or one unlearned he is convinced of all, he is judged of all, and thus all the secrets of his heart made manifest; and so falling down on his face he will worship God, and repeat that God is in you of a truth."
symptoms	• You are not afraid to speak out publicly or take strong stands. • You tend to see needs of the groups as a whole, and are willing to take Scriptural stands on what must be done. • When you speak publicly people are convicted by the truth you give. • You are convincing when you present an answer. • You have a forceful personality.
comment	Those holding the view that the gift of prophecy ceased after the completion of the canon of Scripture but feel that the forth-telling aspect of the gift has been transferred base it on II Peter 2:1 where the Old Testament prophets and teachers of New Testament times are compared. However, one should be cautioned that the analogy is to show that all who claim to give God's message are not what they claim and not to show that the prophetical function has been taken over by teachers. The book is dealing with false teaching.

TEACHING

introduction	The gift of teaching is mentioned in 3 of the 4 passages (exception I Peter 4) on spiritual gifts. In all three places the Greek word, didasko, or inflected form of it is used. In one of the passages (Eph. 4:11) the teaching is modified by a qualifying word, poimena, usually translated by pastor or shepherd. The gift of teaching is fairly well defined in Scriptures. Most interpreters would agree that this gift definitely exists today in the church. No one questions the necessity for the function it serves. The word for teaching, didasko, is used synonymously with other words in the New Testament to describe teaching. These were studied also to help clarify the idea of teaching.

BACKGROUND OF WORDS STUDIED IN CONNECTION WITH GIFT OF TEACHING

Greek (transliteration)	Explanation	Quality in focus	Some typical passages
didasko	This is the usual Greek word for teach. It may mean a discourse with others in order to instruct or a formal lecture.	instruction	Matthew 5 - 7 John 6:59 Acts 18:11 I Cor. 4:17 I Tim. 2:12
manthano	This word has the basic idea of learning. The central idea is the causing of one to learn and follow what he has learned.	acquisition	Matthew 11:29 Matthew 28:19 Acts 14:21
diermeneuo	The central idea is to make truth clear and to effect clarity by explanation.	interpretation (explanation)	Mark 24:27 I Cor. 12:30
ektithemi	The central idea of this word is to set out or place out and signifies the bringing out of latent and secret ideas of a literary passage or system of thought.	exposition	Acts 11:4 Acts 18:26 Acts 28:3
dialegomai	This is used to describe informing by reasoning with	persuasion	Acts 19:9,10

TEACHING (cont.)

definition	A person who has the gift of teaching is one who has the ability to instruct, explain, or expose Biblical truth in such a way as to cause believers of a church to understand the Biblical truth and to acquire the truth for their own use.
comment	It would seem that the methodology used by a teacher could be flexible and would depend in some part upon the way in which the culture best learns truth. For example, Jesus used a great deal of parabolic teaching (see many passages in Gospels). His methodology in teaching offers many principles which could be transferred to other methods of teaching. Paul evidently used a formal one on group lecture method (Acts 20:9) to explain truth as well as teaching through written materials (epistles).
use of the gift	The gift of teaching functions primarily in maturity church growth and can be exercised in large or small groups.
importance of the gift	According to the ranking in I Cor. 12:28 the gift of teaching ranks high among the gifts being included in the leadership gifts. The importance of this gift to the church can be seen when it is recognized that time and time again in the New Testament exhortations to practical living are first preceded by teaching upon which the exhortations are based. Practice must be based upon truth taught.
examples in Scripture showing existence in church	Acts 13:1 "Now there were in the church that was at Antioch certain prophets and teachers; as Barnabas, and Simeon that was called Niger, and Lucius of Cyrene, and Manean, which had been brought up with Herod the tetrarch, and Saul."
example showing results	Acts 19:9,10 "But when divers were hardened, and believed not, but spake evil of that way before the multitude, he departed from them, and separated the disciples, lecturing (dialegomenos) in the school of one Tyrannus. And this continued by the space of two years; so that all they which dwelt in Asia heard the Word of the Lord Jesus, both Jews and Greeks."
example used in gathered church meeting	I Cor. 14:26 "How is it, then, brethren? When ye come in together, every one of you hath a psalm, hath a doctrine (teaching), hath a tongue, hath a revelation, hath an church. Let all things be done unto edifying."

TEACHING (cont.)

example of what teaching should do in a believer	Col. 1:28 "Whom we preach, warning every man, and teaching every man in all wisdom; that we may present every man perfect in Christ Jesus;"
symptoms	• People will constantly understand truth as a result of what you say about the Bible. • You will have a tremendous drive within to understand truth and to see ways to explain it to others. • You will be able to discipline yourself to much study of God's Word. • You will find yourself overly concerned about meaning and will not be satisfied with unclear explanations (either by yourself or others). • You will constantly be improving your methodology in teaching in order to cause learning to take place. • You will see people becoming more Christ-like in their actions and thoughts as a result of your helping them understand and use Biblical truth. • People will know God in ever increasing depth because of your ability to practically explain Biblical truth in terms of today's situation.
caution	Teachers because of their influence over so many will be particularly judged for what they teach others as implied in James 3:2, "My brethren, be not many teachers, knowing that we shall receive the greater condemnation."

PASTORING   synonym: shepherding, oversight, leadership, ruling

introduction   The Ephesians passage on gifts list apostles, prophets, evangelists, and pastors who are teachers as people who will equip the church to do the ministry.   If this list is taken by metonymy to represent gifts then there is a pastoral gift. Some certainly hold this view.   The leader who is known by the name of "pastor" is also synonymously called "elder" and "bishop".   Other terms are used to describe the functions of this leader in basic leadership passages.   Most likely the person who exercises the pastoral gift would be a multi-gifted person as seen in the qualifying phrase (who are teachers), in Paul's comment to Timothy (especially those who teach as well as rule), and in the functions required by the pastoral office.

arriving   I have done the following in trying to arrive at the pastoral gift.
at a   ● studied the "shepherd" concept in the New Testament leadership
definition   passages to understand the implications of it in terms of capacity needed to fulfill it,
             ● studied the role of the "elder" and "bishop" (terms used synonymously to describe the pastor) to see capacities needed to exercise function related to these words,
             ● studied other terms which appear less frequently in connection with the above three and usually describe what these leaders do,
             ● recognized that there is a structural New Testament church office (pastor-bishop-elder) which is necessary to order in the church while at the same time maintaining a distinctiveness between the necessary structure needed and the capacity of the person filling that office.

background   See next page for table of background studies.
studies

definition   The <u>pastoral gift</u> is the capacity to exercise influence over a group so as to lead it toward a goal or purpose with particular emphasis on the capacity to make decisions for, to protect from error, and to disseminate truth primarily by modelling for the purpose of maturing the group toward Christlikeness.

dissenting   Some would classify what I have called the "pastoral gift" not as a gift but as an office only.   The person filling the office is picked for his spiritual qualifications apart from any so called "pastoral gift."   I Tim. 3 and Titus 1 would be used to delineate the qualifications.   Anyone meeting the qualifications could function in the office if called by God. In any case, these people must certainly fill the office so as to exercise the functions described above in the "pastoral gift."

PASTORING (cont.)

example implying functional capacities I Pet 5:2,3	**Feed** the flock of God which is among you taking the <u>oversight</u> of not by constraint, but willingly; not for filthy lucre, but of a ready mind; neither as being lords over God's heritage but being ensamples to the flock.

example implying functional capacities Acts 20:28,29	Take heed therefore unto yourselves, and to all the flock, over the which the Holy Ghost hath made you <u>overseers,</u> to <u>feed</u> the church of God which he hath purchased with his own blood. For I know this, that after my departing shall grievous wolves enter in among you, not sparing the flock.

background studies

LEADERSHIP PASSAGES	WORD USED TO DESCRIBE LEADER	LITERAL RENDERING/ TRANSLATION	CENTRAL THOUGHT OR FUNCTION	CAPACITY MOST LIKELY NEEDED IN FUNCTION
Acts 20: 17-28	presbutero	/elder	unclear	unclear
	episkopo	/bishop	delegated authority from God	ability to exercise influence so that others follow sensing God is in it
	poimaino (verb form)	/shepherd pastor	caring for needs of those under one; especially protecting from harmful influence	ability to sense needs of people and to meet needs; ability to discern error and to lead people to avoid error by counter-acting with truth
Rom. 12:8 I Tim. 3:5 5:17	proistemi	to stand before/ rule, are over you, maintain	to lead or attend to with care and dili-gence	ability to make decision which others may follow and to maintain or-der in these rulings
I Tim. 3:5	epimeomai	to be con-cerned to-wards/take care of	to take care of involving fore-thought and pro-vision	ability to exercise authority over
Heb. 13:7, 17.24	egeomai	chief person of a pro/ vince/rule	command with official authority	ability to command obedience to truth as one accountable to Christ
I Peter 5:1-11	presbutero sum-presbutero poimaino	elder co-elder shepherd	leader take care of by setting the example, lead-by example	ability to command respect because of experience ability to command obedience by force of personal example

PASTORING (cont.)

---

symptoms

- People usually look to you to make decisions.
- People feel you have authority in things concerning the church.
- You are usually picked as the leader in committees, organizations, and like functional groups.
- You seem to influence the actions of groups by what you do and what you say.
- You have the ability to maintain order or discipline among people.
- You easily see the problems of groups you are related to and accept responsibility to help them.
- You are concerned that groups of Christian that you relate to grow in Christlikeness and unity and are willing to do something about it.
- You would be considered by most (if they were asked) that you are a leader.
- You exert influence over people so as to instill loyalty to you and your way of thinking and doing things.

---

ruling

I have included the passages that deal with ruling (Rom 12:8, I Tim 3:5, 5:17) under the gift of pastor. That means I am not specifying a separate gift of leadership but am assuming that the qualities for ruling are part of the pastoral gift. Some would define a separate gift called leadership. However, I have made my choice on the basis that such an important gift would almost certainly be listed among the leadership gifts which are grouped in I Cor. 12 and those grouped in Eph. 4.

```
WORD OF KNOWLEDGE      synonym:  knowledge
WORD OF WISDOM         synonym:  wisdom
```

introduction	The gifts called Word of Knowledge and Word of Wisdom do not appear by those names in other parallel passages on gifts. Neither are there direct commands nor direct identification of these gifts in illustrations. Several possible illustrations of these gifts do occur in Scripture but there is no "hard evidence" that in fact these are illustrations of these gifts. Whatever definitions are formulated must come solely from a study of the phraseology involved and in the case of wisdom from general teaching on the concept of wisdom as used by God in the Scriptures. These gifts are treated together because of the similarity of the function suggested by the common wording "word of."
some possible assumptions	• These two descriptions are really one. That is, knowledge and wisdom are being used synonymously. The phrases are repeated for emphasis.
	• The two—word of knowledge and word of wisdom—are really not distinct gifts alone but are simply ways in which some of the other gifts such as prophecy or exhortation are exercised.
	• These two are distinct gifts in their own right though there may not be enough evidence to finely distinguish between the two. One can certainly offer tentative definitions which are backed by possible illustrations.
	• The use of logos prefacing both wisdom and knowledge suggests that these gifts are situational communications given by the Spirit for that moment. Thus we are not just talking about people who are knowledgeable about the Bible or God but are talking about a word which comes from God as knowledge or wisdom for a certain specific situation.
	The latter two implications received more weight.

background word studies on Wisdom

Greek	Etymological or literal rendering	Translated by English Word(s)	Central thought
sophia	clear	wisdom	intellectual power backed by moral considerations; some connotations toward skillful use of this power
	Related Words		
	sunesis	intelligence	
	sophidzo	to make wise, to invent, or devise	
	sophos	skilled, clever	
	sunetos	intelligence	

WORD OF KNOWLEDGE (cont.)
WORD OF WISDOM

On Knowledge

Greek	Etymological or literal rendering	Translated by English Word(s)	Central Thought
gnosis		knowledge science	knowledge (connotation= seeking to know, inquiry or investigation)

Related Words

gnosko	to know
gnome	mind
gnosidzo	hath made known have declared
gnostes	expert
gnostos	acquaintance known

definitions   The gift word of knowledge represents the capacity to receive supernaturally revealed knowledge which otherwise could not or would not be known.

definition   The gift word of wisdom represents the capacity to know the mind of the Spirit in a given situation and to communicate clearly the situation, facts, truth, or application of facts and truth to meet the need of the situation.

situational   The exercise of both these gifts is thus situationally specific
specific   and depends upon sensitivity to the Holy Spirit in the unique situation.

use   It would seem entirely feasible that the Gifts Word of Wisdom and Word of Knowledge could be exercised in conjunction with any of the speaking gifts (as a complimentary aspect of the gift) either by the speaker or by some hearer who is led to see the value of what is said in terms of some needful situation.
               It has been the experience of groups which recognize these gifts to see particularly the gift word of knowledge used in conjunction with the revealing of knowledge concerning healing.

possible   Acts 15:19-21 could be an illustration of wisdom since it is
Biblical   clear that the Holy Spirit gave the solution to this
example   situational problem and it is highly likely that James was able
wisdom   to see how to grasp all that had been said and done in terms of a "word of wisdom" for the group.

WORD OF KNOWLEDGE, WISDOM (cont.)

Jas 3:13-18	This passage gives Biblical tether for kinds of "words" of wisdom which are given.

possible Biblical examples of word of knowledge	• Acts 5:3ff Peter's knowledge of God's supernatural judgment. • Acts 16:28 Paul's knowledge of the jailer's suicide. • Acts 18:9 Paul's confirmation to stay on at Corinth. • Acts 20:25 Paul's affirmation that he will never see Ephesian elders again. (Possibly also verses 29,30). • Acts 21:10 Knowledge in conjunction with prophecy. • Acts 27:22-26 Knowledge of shipwreck without loss of life.

present example of word of knowledge	John Wimber of the Vineyard Christian Fellowship of Yorba Linda, California, manifests the gift of word of knowledge. In his case God gives him knowledge that he could not possibly otherwise know in 5 different ways. • He sees it like Newspaper headlines in his mind. • He hears it in an audible-like inner voice. • He sees a picture of it. • In healing situations he actually feels the pain in the organ or part of the body in which the like situation is present in a person. • Rarely, he opens his mouth and out it comes without prior consciousness of it. His gift, word of knowledge, is used in a complimentary fashion with a healing ministry as well as for other purposes.

symptoms of word of wisdom gift	• The unusual sensitivity to the Holy Spirit which allows recognition of His promptings in terms of ideas and concepts. • The quickness to transfer concepts to application in situations. • A good understanding of spiritual truth in the Word. • An ability to see principles of truth. • An intuitive quickly grasped situation with a clear possible solution to the situation. The solution appears almost instantaneously. Later analysis and evaluation will confirm the intuitive solution. • When a word of wisdom comes the "intuitive-like solution" is usually authenticated by those who hear it with a consensus approval.

symptoms of word of knowledge gift	• An ususual sensitivity to the Holy Spirit which recognizes that thoughts or impressions are from the Spirit. • A recognition that in certain situations in which the Spirit wants to work you have knowledge that you know you could not have originated yourself (information beyond your experience on some given situation). • An awareness that physical feelings may be correlated to something the Spirit wants to communicate.

EXHORTATION

introduction	Much information is given in the New Testament about the gift of exhortation. We know it is a distinct gift and **not** simply a part of the gift of prophecy since both are listed in Romans 12 separately. Many illustrations of this gift abound in the epistles showing that its function is very important to the life of the church.

background
word
studies   On Exhortation

Greek word	Etymological or literal use	Basic idea	Contextual verification
parakaleo	to call to a person	1. to beseech or admonish one to pursue some specific course of conduct in the future	Acts 2:40 Romans 15:30 Romans 16:17 I Cor. 1:10 II Cor. 9:5 I Thess. 4:1 Heb. 1:25
		2. to comfort one in terms of some trial being experienced or already experienced	II Cor. 1:4 Eph. 6:22 Col. 4:8 I Thess. 4:18 I Thess. 5:11
		3. to encourage generally in order that people might face future events which may arise	Acts 11:23 Acts 14:22 I Cor. 14:31

definition	The **gift of exhortation** is the capacity to urge people to action in terms of applying Scriptural truth, or to encourage people generally with Scriptural truth, or to comfort people through application of Scriptural truths to their needs.

comments	A person possessing this gift will normally be stronger in exercising one of the aspects of it: • to urge or admonish • to encourage • to comfort However full development of the gift will see all aspects of the gift used both privately and publicly.

EXHORTATION (cont.)

example of exhortation urging to action	"NowI urge you brethren, by our Lord Jesus Christ and by the love of the Spirit to strive together with me in your prayers to God for me" Romans 15:30.
example of exhortation encouraging others	"Then when he had come and witnessed the grace of God, he rejoiced and began to encourage them all with resolute heart to remain true to the Lord" Acts 11:23.
example of exhortation comforting others	"Blessed be the God...the Father of mercies and God of all comfort who comforteth us in all our affliction, that we may be able to comfort them that are in any affliction, through the comfort where we ourselves are comforted" II Cor. 1:3,4.
symptoms of this gift	• People generally react strongly (sometimes for and sometimes against) what you say. • You frequently advise others to do this or that. • You share a word with someone in need such that he takes the word as a comforting word from God. • People frequently confide in you their innermost problems because they sense in you an empathetic ear and by such confiding are comforted. • People like to be around you because you cheer them up simply by your attitude and demeanor. • You often sense an urgency to get something done and are willing to transmit this urgency to others. • You love to share with anyone a truth from a verse of Scripture which has meant much to you. • You are not satisfied with a superficial acceptance of truth but seek to have people actually use it. • You enjoy sharing particular aspects of your testimony with others because you know God will use it in the lives of others.
uses	The gift of exhortation is the major way through which God allows the body to enable each other to live practical Christian lives. Christians encourage each other to face trials by sharing what God has done for them in similar situations. Christians urge each other to action in terms of practical application. Christians are encouraged to look forward to what lies ahead. These kinds of things take place when the exhortive gift is exercised on a one to one basis, a one to few, few to one, one to many basis. It is a gift which can be exercised both privately and publicly. It is a gift which quite a few people in any given assembly can expect to have and should use.

TONGUES   synonym: kinds of tongues
INTERPRETATION OF TONGUES

---

introduction   The gift of tongues was a "problem" gift. In the Corinthian
church it was divisive and was a strong factor in nurturing
spiritual pride. Or rather the abuse of the gift brought about
the ill-desired effects. Because of this problem Paul wrote
three chapters on gifts in I Corinthians. Much of what we know
about gifts occurs in these three chapters written to deal with
a problem associated with one gift. In Acts the gift of
tongues was given several times by the Holy Spirit. In one
case, Acts 2, the men who received the gift of tongues spoke in
"other" recognizable dialects. In Acts 10:46 either the gift
of tongues was again "other" recognizable dialects, or Peter
and his friends had the gift of interpretation for they heard
them "magnify God". In Acts 19:6 it is unclear whether the
tongues were understood or not. In each of the above incidents
concerning tongues the primary purpose of the gift was to
authenticate that new segments being added to the church were
God's own work and hence certainly met with his approval.

---

basic   When Paul mentions the gift of tongues he calls it kinds of
word   tongues. The word kinds (genos) can mean offspring, family,
studies   stock, race, sort, species. The word tongues (glossa) is used
to describe the common tongue in the mouth and by metonymy can
mean anything spoken by that tongue. It is used by way of
metonymy when describing the gift of tongues. It is not clear
whether the utterances are always a known dialect or <u>not</u>. It
is clear however that the utterances are <u>not</u> known to the one
doing the speaking, unless he also has the gift of
interpretation. In the Acts 2 passage the word dialektos
(indicating a recognizable language) is used synonymously with
glossa. In other Acts passages dialektos is <u>not</u> used. The
word interpretation in interpretation of tongues is the word
hermeneuo. This word is used to describe the process of
explaining something to someone who does <u>not</u> understand it and
to describe the process of translating from one language to the
other.

---

definition   The <u>gift of tongues</u> is an ability given spontaneously by the
Holy Spirit to an individual to speak in a language unknown to
the speaker.

The gift, <u>interpretation of tongues</u>, is a gift whereby a
believer is given an ability spontaneously by the Holy Spirit
to translate the utterances of one using the gift of tongues.

TONGUES
INTERPRETATION OF TONGUES (cont.)

---

examples

Acts 2:4 "And they were all filled with the Holy Ghost, and began to speak with other tongues, as the Spirit gave them utterance."

Acts 10:45,46 "And they of the circumcision which believed were astonished, as many as came with Peter, because that on the Gentiles also was poured out the gift of the Holy Ghost, for they heard them speak with tongues and magnify God."

Acts 19:6 "And when Paul had laid his hands upon them the Holy Ghost came on them; and they spake with tongues, and prophesied."

---

use of tongues

- Tongues were used to authenticate the addition of non-Jewish people into God's church (Acts 2, 10, 19) and thus to show that God's church was to be universal.
- Tongues are primarily used as a sign to unbelievers rather than believers (I Cor. 14:22).
- Tongues are secondarily used for edification in the gathered church (I Cor. 14:22, 26, 27).

---

use of interpretation of tongues

In public meetings the use of the gift of tongues should be orderly (not more than a few and these one at a time) and should allow for the use of the gift of interpretation in order that all be edified (I Cor. 14:26,27).

---

when tongues should not be used

Tongues should not be used in public meetings of the gathered church unless there is one present who can interpret and thus bring edification to all present.

---

symptoms

It would seem that this gift, given spontaneously, is not a gift which can be developed. You either have this gift or you don't. Those holding to the concept of "gift contagion" would say that the gift could be caught--i.e. influenced by people with the gift so as to stimulate the acceptance of the gift.

---

caution

Whether or not these gifts exist today is a question all its own apart from the definition of the gifts. There does not seem to be exegetical evidence showing cessation of the gift (indeed a passing comment by Paul says forbid not to speak in tongues). Many do not feel that the genuine New Testament gift of tongues is present today. However, many today use this gift and manifest it according to New Testament practice.

DISCERNMENT   synonym: discerning of spirits

---

introduction   In the early church there was no finalized form of the New Testament such as exists today for our use. God used prophets, teachers, and other of the leadership gifts to reveal truth and explain truth and apply truth to the early believers. It is clear from II Cor. 11:13, II Peter 2:1, I John 4:1-3, and Jude 4 that there were false apostles and teachers and others claiming to have authority from God. The gift of discernment was God's gift to the church to protect it from these false prophets, teachers, apostles, etc. One having this gift was able "to try the spirits," that is, prove the source from which so called truth came and hence to distinguish between truth and error. Peter warns in his second epistle that this ability to discern error, particularly from teachers, will be a growing need in the church. Hebrews 5:14 amplifies the function of discernment more broadly to good and evil and indicates that such discernment is the mark of maturity.

---

basic word   On Discernment
studies

Greek	Etymological or literal rendering	English words	Central Idea (s)	Verses
diakrisis	probably from a word used to describe an act of severing through something to form two distinct parts	disputations discerning discern	a separation or distinction a discerning, the act of it, or the faculty to do so	Rom. 14:1 Heb. 5:14

	Related Words		
	diakrino	to separate, sever Acts 15:9 to make a distinction or difference I Cor. 11:29 to make to differ, I Cor 4:7 distinguish, prefer, confer a superiority, to examine, scrutinize I Cor 11:31 estimate, evaluate I Cor 14:29 to discern, discriminate Matt. 16:3 to judge, to decide I Cor 6:5 to distinguish, or	
	anakrino	separate out so as to investigate	
	apokoino	a judicial decision, a sentence	
	apokrisis	a response or answer	
	epikrino	to adjudge or give sentence	
	Synonym		
	dokimadzo	to test, prove, so as to decide I John 4:1	

DISCERNMENT   (cont.)

definition	The gift of discernment is the analytical capacity to distinguish truth from non-truth by judging the truth or non-truth in terms of revealed truth or principles taken from that truth. In its widest sense it is the judgment between right and wrong.
example	Hebrews 5:14 "But strong meat belongeth to them that are of full age, even those who by reason of use have their senses exercised to discern (diakrisin) both good and evil."
example	I John 4:1-3 "Beloved, believe not every spirit, but try the spirits whether they be of God: because many false prophets are gone out into the world." Here spirit is used by metonymy to indicate teachings prompted by a spirit. The idea being, you must judge the teaching as to its source—the Holy Spirit or other spirits. This example could also be expanded to include the concept of discerning of spirits which are at the source of any situation. One who had the gift of discerning of spirits would be able to identify the spirit which is the source of some problem.
example	I Cor. 14:29 "let the prophets speak two or three, and let the other judge (diakrinetosan)."
example modern	Many writers seem to evidence this gift in the present church. For example note the many writings dealing with applied ecclesiology in which the church as presently existing is being critically examined in the light of Scriptural teaching. Another example of this gift in action is seen in the ministry of Francis Schaeffer. A.W. Tozer also exemplifed this gift.
use	• In the early church to distinguish truth from non-truth in terms of verbal utterances. • In the church possessing the Scriptures to discern if explanatory truth is on target. • To protect the church (local, regional, and universal) from heretical tendencies in teaching or in practice.
symptoms	• A keen sense for recognizing inconsistencies. • The tendency to always be figuring out what is wrong with something or how it can be improved. • The ability to categorize. • The ability to think in logical steps. • A good grasp of Scriptural truth in general. • You often and usually quickly notice when public speakers give wrong interpretations, or misapply Scripture. • A deep underlying spirit of conviction which will not allow you to rest when you know people are being given half-truth, misapplied truth, or false teaching, and are asked to act upon it.

FAITH   synonym: gift of prayer

introduction	Concerning the gift of faith very little is mentioned in the Scriptures. If it were <u>not</u> for its inclusion in the list of gifts in I Corinthians 12 one would probably <u>not</u> identify it as a gift. However, it is included as a special gift given to some to edify the church. Therefore it is distinct from faith which each of us must have to be saved and to walk with God. Such faith is a fruit of the Spirit and should be a growing part of every believer's walk with God. But that there is a gift of faith beyond that which is the fruit of the Spirit is clear from the I Corinthians passage. Since there is little or no reference to the gift in terms of illustration of its use or command to exercise it, the definition which follows is simply a logical extension implied in a study of the word "faith". Of course any such interpretation, as logical as it may be, where backed only by the silence of Scripture should not be presented dogmatically as "the truth" but as a good possible explanation of the truth.
background word study	The word for "faith" used in I Corinthians 12:9 is the word pistis, the common word which along with the verb form pisteuo is used frequently in Scripture. The basic uses of the word include,

- trust,
- trustworthiness,
- the assurance or basis for faith,
- a pledge of faith,
- by metonymy for what is believed.

definition	The <u>gift of faith</u> is that unusual capacity to recognize in a given situation that which God intends to do perhaps generally and to <u>trust</u> Him for it until He brings it to pass. It is most likely expressed through prayer with God (i.e. the prayer of faith) though it may simply be a belief in a vision of what God can and will do in some situation.
example in O.T.	Romans 4 speaks of Abraham as a man of faith. His unusual ability to believe God's promises is praised by Paul. According to Romans 4:20, "yet, looking unto the promise of God, he wavered not through unbelief, but waxed strong through faith, giving glory to God." Abraham received a promise or vision of what God intended to do. He believed that God would bring it to pass and God did and is doing so. Though an Old Testament example of faith it illustrates the concept.
example in N.T. church	Paul, several times in his ministry as revealed in the book of Acts, seems to display evidence of the gift of faith. He received in his unusual call a vision of what he was to do for God (see Acts 9:15,26:16-20) and he clung to this vision throughout his lifetime (see II Tim. 4:7,8). Further illustrations in Paul's life include his Macedonian call (Acts 16), his unshakable assurance that God would have him witness before kings and rulers in Jerusalem and Rome (Acts 21:9-14, 26:19, 23:11, 28:14), his experience at Corinth in which God revealed to him what would happen and gave assurance (Acts 18:10,11), his unusual experience in the ship (Acts 27:22-26).

FAITH (cont.)

modern example	A most probable example in modern church history is the example of George Mueller of Bristol. This man time and time again believed God for provision for his orphanages and for the needs of Christians all over the world. In answer to prayer to God over $7,000,000 was given to the Lord's work under George Mueller. Here are Mueller's words. "I myself have for twenty-nine years been waiting for an answer to prayer concerning a certain spiritual blessing. Day by day I have been enabled to continue in prayer for this blessing. At home and abroad, in this country and in foreign lands, in health and in sickness, however much occupied I have been enabled, day by day, by God's help to bring this matter before Him; and still I have <u>not</u> the full answer yet. Nevertheless, I look for it. I expect it confidently. The very fact that day after day, and year after year, for twenty-nine years, the Lord has enabled me to continue, patiently, believingly, to wait on Him for the blessing, still further encourages me to wait on; and so fully am I assured that God hears me about this matter, that I have often been enabled to praise Him beforehand for the full answer, which I shall ultimately receive to my prayers on this subject. Thus, you see, dear reader, that while I have hundreds, yea, thousands of answers, year by year, I have also, like yourself and other believers, the trial of faith concerning certain matters."

symptoms	• An unusual desire to accept God's promises at face value and to apply them to given situations until God fulfills them. • Receiving what you believe to be a vision of some future work of God and trusting God for it until it comes to pass. • The recurring experience in the midst of situations to sense that God is going to do something unusual even though most around you do <u>not</u> have this kind of assurance. • The recurring experiencing of the prayer of faith—that is, time and time again, the praying for something only once and receiving assurance that your prayer has been heard and answered though long periods of time may elapse before seeing the answer. • An unusual desire to know God in fullness and to be cast on him and him alone for solutions to problems. • The thrill of knowing time and time again that God is real because he and he alone has specifically and in a detailed way answered your prayer requests. • An attitude: <u>not</u> only that God "can" but that he "will" and already "has done so" in various crises situations.

uses of the gift	The gift of faith is used by God • to bring glory to Himself (i.e. to reveal himself as He really is to people). • to exhort the church to pray and believe in a prayer answering God. • to meet crisis needs in the church and individual lives.

GIVING

introduction	Because giving and sharing are so much a part of every Christian's responsibility it is hard to recognize that there is a gift called giving which uniquely belongs to only some Christians. But we know this to be true for Paul lists the gift of giving along with other well-known gifts such as teaching and prophecy in Romans 12. His qualifying descriptive phrase in Romans 12:8 forms the basis for the descriptive definition of the gift of giving.

basic
word studies   On Giving

Greek	Etymological or literal rendering	English translation	Central Thought	Verses
metadidomi	to give by sharing	give impart distribute	to give or share with others to meet their needs (connotation=especially of excess goods)	Rom. 12:8 Eph. 4:28 Luke 3:11

Related words

didomi	to give
diadidomi	to give throughout
apodidomi	to give away from oneself
epididomi	to give upon or over to, completely
paradidomi	to give over to
anadidomi	to hand over

Synonym

doreomai	to give as a gift

Qualifying phrase

en aploteti	with liberality	II Cor. 8:2,9: 11,13
	with purity	II Cor. 11:3
	in sincerity	Col 3:22

definition	The gift of giving is the capacity to give liberally to meet the needs of others and yet to do so with a purity of motive which senses that the giving is a simple sharing of that which God has provided.

GIVING (cont.)

example	Acts 4:34-37 "Neither was there any among them that lacked: for as many as were possessors of lands or houses sold them, and brought the prices of the things that were sold, and laid them down at the apostles' feet: and distribution was made unto every man according as he had need. And Joses, who by the apostles was surnamed Barnabas, (which is being interpreted, the son of consolation), a Levite, and of the country of Cyprus, having land, sold it, and brought the money and laid it at the apostles' feet."
example modern day	George Mueller of Bristol in conjunction with the exercising of his gift of faith saw God supply over $7,000,000. Much of this was given to foreign missions and home missions. At the first of each year Mueller began his work with little or no money on hand. Almost all that came in during a year was used for his orphanage or sent on to home or foreign missions. He was simply a channel through whom God sent money.
use	• To meet the needs of believers within your own assembly (Eph. 4:28, Gal. 6:10, I John 3:17, I Tim. 5:33ff). • To meet the needs of believers of other assemblies (II Cor. 8,9; Romans 15:25,26). • To meet the needs of those persons exercising leadership gifts on a full-time basis (Phil. 4:10, Gal. 6:9, I Cor. 9:1-11, I Tim. 6:16). • To meet the needs of non-believers (Gal. 6:10).
symptoms	• A sensitivity to recognize material needs of others. • A quickness to assume some burden for meeting the needs of others when you sense they have a need. • A relative freedom from a "me first attitude". • A capacity because of position or job so that you have means to give. • Abilities which can be used by God to amass financial resources. • A carefulness in the handling of your financial matters along with a bent toward obtaining only those things which you need. • A conviction that all of what you have belongs to God and you as a steward want to be a channel for God to use what he has given you.
comment	Don't in your thinking limit this gift to "rich" people. The Macedonian Christians were poor people but God gave this "liberal spirit of giving" to them. And he said they gave beyond their means. They gave and he supplied, and supplied, and supplied. George Mueller is another case in point. He was not a rich businessman, but a full-time Christian totally dependent on God to meet his own needs. This God did but because of the "liberality of giving" which Mueller possessed, God gave beyond his needs and he in turn "relayed" it on to needs which his sensitive spirit picked up.

FEEDBACK ON MATURITY GIFTS

question   Match the gifts given below with their definition or key words from
           definitions or uses or symptoms by placing the number of the gift in
           the blank beside the definition, key word, use, or symptom.

1. prophecy   7. tongues
2. teaching   8. interpretation of tongues
3. pastoring   9. discernment
4. word of knowledge   10. faith
5. word of wisdom   11. giving
6. exhortation

_____a.   capacity to expound publicly to exhort, edify, or console
_____b.   associated with knowing the mind of the Spirit in a given situation
_____c.   urge people to action, or comfort, or encourage
_____d.   basically a capacity to exercise influence over a group to lead it
          toward a goal
_____e.   capacity to instruct, explain, or expose Biblical truth in such a way
          as to cause people to understand
_____f.   used to encourage each other to face trials or to comfort in the
          midst of a trial
_____g.   one symptom--you are not afraid to speak out publicly or take a
          strong stand on an issue
_____h.   one symptom--you seem to influence the actions of groups of which
          you are a part both by what you do and what you say
_____i.   used to edify the group by explaining what someone has spoken in
          tongues
_____j.   given spontaneously by the Holy Spirit enabling one to speak in a
          language unknown to the speaker
_____k.   capacity to recognize in a given situation that which God intends to
          do and to trust Him for it until He brings it to pass
_____l.   one symptom - a keen sense for recognizing inconsistencies
_____m.   one symptom - an unusual sensitivity to the Holy Spirit which allows
          recognition of His promptings in terms of truth being revealed which
          others do not have
_____n.   this gift is not to be used if the interpretation of tongues gift is
          not available
_____o.   capacity to give liberally to meet the needs of others and yet do so
          with a purity of motive
_____p.   one symptom--a conviction that all of what you have belongs to God
          and you as a steward want to be a channel for God to provide the
          material needs of others
_____q.   one symptom--an unusual desire to accept God's promises at face
          value and to apply them to given situations until God meets the
          situation
_____r.   an analytical capacity to distinguish truth from non-truth
_____s.   one symptom--you would be considered by most (if they were asked)
          that you are a leader

answers   1 a.   4 b.   6 c.   3 d.   2 e.   6 f.   1 g.

          3 h.   8 i.   7 j.   10 k.   9 l.   5 m.   7 n.

          11 o.   11 p.   10 q.   9 r.   3 s.

GIFTS FOCUSED ON NUMERICAL CHURCH GROWTH

introduction   The following five gifts are primarily used in outreach either
to demonstrate God's concern, to reach new people with God's
salvation message and persuade them to begin lives of
discipleship, or to authenticate God's message so they will
believe it.

LIST OF NUMERICAL CHURCH GROWTH GIFTS

5 gifts
with
outward
focus

Gifts	Basic Thrust	Exercised with	
		Regional church	Local church
apostleship	reaching and formulating new people into local churches	x	
	initiating new Christian organizations which will help carry out needed tasks being overlooked	x	x
evangelism	reaching new people	x	x
miracles	authentication of God's message	x	x
healing	authentication of God's message	x	x
mercy	demonstration of God's love	x	x

APOSTLESHIP

introduction	Some would <u>not</u> classify apostleship as a gift but would confine it to an office filled by those who were handpicked by Jesus to function in a foundational role in instigating the church. One holding this view would say then that with the passing away of the twelve (most would include Paul as a special case) this function ceased to exist. Others would agree that there was a special office called apostleship which did in fact exist only in New Testament times and that this office was filled by the original 12 (and Paul). They would also agree that this office did cease with the death of the 12 (and Paul). However, they would add that there is an apostleship gift distinct from the original authoritative apostolic office. This gift continued beyond the first century. There is ample evidence that there was a functional apostolic role filled by a number of named individuals in the Scriptures beyond Paul and the Twelve which does in fact meet the requirement of a gift of apostleship.
basic word studies	On Apostleship

Greek (Transliteration)	Etymological or literal rendering	Basic idea	English translation	Contextual confirmation
apostolos	one sent forth apo, from + stello, to send	one who acts authorita- tively for another	apostle messenger	Heb. 3:1 Luke 6:13, 9:10 Acts 14:4,14 Romans 16:7 II Cor. 8:23 Phil. 2:25 I Thess. 2:6
apostole	a sending	a mission a ministry	apostle- ship	Acts 1:25 Romans 1:5 I Cor. 9:2 Gal. 2:8

definition	The <u>gift of apostleship</u> refers to a special leadership capacity in which one exerts influence over others so as to establish new local churches and new works needed to enhance the spread of Christianity. Further, this gift functions to guide these new works in their foundational stages.
explanation	The capacity to establish new local churches and other necessary Christian structures necessitates a special kind of authority. This is sometimes referred to as a "call" from God. The one having this special authoritative influence is usually recognized by a local church as having authority from God to perform the task of pioneer work. The gift can be exercised within ones own culture or cross-culturally. Traditionally the apostolic gift has been associated with missionary work since its pioneer-quality was immediately evident. However, all who "go" as missionaries certainly don't have this gift, and

APOSTLESHIP (cont.)

explanation cont	many who "stay" should recognize this gift and apply it to "pioneer situations" within their own locality.
examples	Acts 13:1-3 "Now there were in the church that was at Antioch certain prophets and teachers; as Barnabas, and Simeon that was called Niger, and Lucius of Cyrene, and Manaen, which had been brought up with Herod the tetrarch and Saul. As they ministered to the Lord, and fasted, the Holy Spirit said, Separate me Barnabas, and Saul for the work whereunto I have called them. And when they had fasted and prayed, and laid their hands on them, they sent them away." Note Barnabas as well as Paul was included in this apostolic gift.
	Acts 14:4, 14 "But the multitude of the city was divided: and part held with the Jews, and part with the apostles. Which when the apostles, Barnabas and Paul, heard of, they rent their clothes, and ran in among the people, crying out, "...
	Acts 14:22,23 "Confirming to the souls of the disciples, and exhorting them to continue in the faith, and that we must through much tribulation enter into the kingdom of God. And when they had ordained them elders in every church, and had prayed with fasting, they commended them to the Lord, on whom they believed."
negative example	II Cor. 11:13 "For such are false prophets, deceitful workers, transforming themselves into the apostles of Christ." The value of this passage is that it implies there are many who were exercising this gift (though some were not true apostles).
example establishing leadership	Titus 1:5 "For this cause left I thee in Crete, that thou shouldest set in order the things that are wanting, and ordain elders in every city, as I had appointed thee:"
example	I Thess. 2:6 "Nor of men sought we glory, neither of you, nor yet of others, when we might have been burdensome, as the apostles of Christ." This use of apostles refers to Paul and Silvannus and Timothy.
example	Rom. 16:7 "Salute Andronicus and Junia, my kinsmen, and my fellow prisoners, who are of note among the apostles, who also were in Christ before me." (note: Junia might possibly be a woman's name)

APOSTLESHIP (cont.)

---

use

- founding of new church structures: it is through this sending-forth effort of selected individuals by established churches that new churches are founded. The individuals thus selected for this role must sense the God-given ability for this role as well as those doing the sending forth.

- founding of new mission structures: it is through apostolic gifted people that God has historically raised up structures to spur on the mission movement and to bring renewal into church structures which have lost their vision.

---

symptoms

- A strong sense of call by God for establishing new works.
- An equally strong confirmation by the local church of which you are a part.
- A forceful personality which can trust God to do what is necessary in unusual situations in order to establish authority for God's work.
- Usually will be a multi-gifted person having one or more other leadership gifts beyond apostleship.
- Ability to face new situations.
- A clear understanding of the nature of the church and its purpose.
- A personality which attracts people to follow (usually forceful).
- A person who can sense what God wants to do and is not afraid to try.
- A drive within which cannot be satisfied apart from seeing people presently unreached being reached and included in a community of God's people.

---

special
comment

Watchman Nee holds a distinct view concerning this gift (which he would call an office). For a view worthy of thought see his book The Normal Christian Church Life, p. 17 ff.

EVANGELISM

introduction	The church expands numerically by seeing people converted to Christianity. New people primarily become disciples through exercise of this gift. It is ranked third in order of strategic importance behind apostleship and prophecy.
basic word studies	Because of the length of the table on word studies it is attached following this map on Evangelism.
definition	The gift of evangelism in general refers to the capacity to confront people publicly and privately through various communicative methods with the message of salvation in Christ so as to see them respond by taking initial steps in Christian discipleship.
one aspect of this gift	In the regional church the gift of evangelism is related to the apostolic function of proclaiming publicly and privately with authoritative power the message of Christ concerning salvation to people who have not heard or understood so as to cause them to respond by taking initial steps in Christian discipleship.
example public challenge	Peter's ministry as seen in Acts 2,4,5 and 10 illustrates this aspect of evangelism. Philip's ministry in Acts 8:5-13 and verse 40 illustrates this aspect. Paul's ministry in Acts 16:9-15 and many other passages also illustrates this aspect of evangelism.
example private persuasion	Philip's ministry to the Ethiopian Eunich in Acts 8:26-39 and Paul's ministry to the Philippian jailer in Acts 16:25-33 illustrate the evangelistic gift used with individuals.
second aspect of this gift	In the regional church the gift of evangelism is one of the leadership gifts mentioned. Besides direct outreach to unsaved it is used to encourage members of local churches to exercise their gifts of evangelism. That is, the evangelist is to influence or lead Christians to evangelize.
example	A careful reading of Ephesian 4:11,12 shows that the leadership gifts mentioned have as their primary focus the enabling of the individual Christians to perform ministries according to their individual gifts.
third aspect of this gift	At local church level the gift of evangelism involves the capacity to confront men and women in everyday life and so influence them through exemplary lives and verbal explanation for those lives so as to cause people to respond by taking initial steps of Christian discipleship.

EVANGELISM   (cont)

uses

The gift of evangelism is the primary means of God's reconciling men and women to himself. It causes numeric growth in the Church and introduces people to the discipleship process.

symptoms

symptoms of this gift include,

- the ability to talk before large groups or converse easily with strangers or people of short acquaintance (public aspect)
- the ability to persuade or influence people (public or private aspect)
- an intense spirit of unrest within at the thought of people being unsaved and eternally unreconciled to God
- the ability to insert spiritual truth in normal conversation with unsaved by sensing occasions to do so
- a freedom and joy in talking about Christian things naturally and unforced
- the fact that unsaved people with whom you come in contact often end up by pursuing further what Christianity is all about
- the fact that unsaved people actually make discipleship commitments as a direct result or indirect result of your influence
- the fact that you specifically pray much for unsaved people by name
- the fact that you specifically pray much for large groups of people
- the ability to make friends easily

Related maps   see Chart on Evangelism Word studies, p. 80

WORD STUDIES ON EVANGELISM AND RELATED WORDS

Greek	Etymological or literal	English word(s)	Central Idea(s)	Verses
evan-gelistes	from evangelion	evangelist	one who gave the salvation message to unsaved people	Acts 5:42

Cognate Words

evan-gelidzo	bring good	preach, bring good news	to give forth and explain the salvation message to both individuals and groups	Acts 5:42 8:4,12,25 35,40 13:22
evan-gelion	reward for bringing good news before + announce	gospel, glad tidings preached before	news of salvation provided in Christ to announce in advance	Acts 15:7 Gal. 3:8

Related Words to Evangelistic Communication

laleo	utter	speak, tell utter	speak to people (about Christ)	Acts 4:1
didasko	learn	teach	explain clearly the message about Christ	Acts 4:1 5:21
kerusso		preach publish proclaim	to cry or proclaim as a herald (used only with apostolic functioning)	Acts 8:5,6 10:42 20:25
kata-ngello	down + messenger	preach show teach	announce publicly to tell thoroughly	Acts 4:2 13:5 15:36
martureo	witness something	bare record witness testify	to give a witness to	Acts 23:11
dia-martureo		may testify witness charge	to give a solemn witness to (heavy emotional connotation)	Acts 18:5
dia-legomai	intensive pronoun + estimate	disputed reasoned preached spoke	to consider something thoroughly by discussing it or to reason carefully within oneself	Acts 17:2 18:4 19:8

MIRACLES   synonym: operation of power

introduction	I Corinthians 12:10 gives the only direct information about this gift. The words describing this gift are words which usually mean powerful workings. Often these works are attributed to God. Paul in referring to his own powerful workings says that what he did was used as a sign that his work was of God (see II Cor. 12:12). Primarily then the gift of miracles was an authenticity gift giving credence to the message of the early witnesses of the gospel. The question of the existence of this gift today is disputed. Those claiming non-existence of the gift say that it was needed in the first century to establish authority of the message of the Gospel but is not needed today. Yet others, especially those associated with missionary work among animistic tribes, feel this authenticity gift does in fact exist today and is needed to establish the authority of the Gospel among unreached people.
definition	The <u>working of miracles</u> is a gift in which the person exercising the gift invokes the miraculous intervention of God to a given situation with the result that God receives recognition for the supernatural intervention.

Table of Possible Examples Associated with This Gift

Passages	Who	Incident	Result
Acts 4:33	Apostles	refers to healing of lame man and like miracles	gave authenticity to apostle's message on resurrection of Jesus
Acts 5:12	Peter	judgment of Ananias	people respected the authority of Peter
Acts 6:8	Stephen	unnamed miracles	Stephen had much influence synagogues
Acts 8:5-7	Philip	unclean spirits cast out, lame healed	people heeded carefully what Philip said
Acts 3:9-12	Paul	power encounter with Elymas the sorcerer	Sergius Paulus heeded Paul's witness and became a Christian
Acts 16:16-18	Paul	demon possessed maiden	Girl freed of demon
Heb. 2:3		summary passage	shows "authenticity" aspect of miracles

symptoms	• God will put you in positions in which you must see the power of God demonstrated in order to vindicate his character. • You have a sense of the presence of the power of God in given situations and are willing to be God's channel (risk involved) to accomplish great things.
use	The gift of miracles, if the above examples do refer to this gift, seems to be used to validate claims to the authenticity of the Gospel message and its messengers. The missiological concept of "power encounter" involves the use of this gift.

HEALING   syn: gifts of healings

introduction	The gift of healing, one of the so-called miraculous gifts, is a gift over which there is disagreement. Some would say that the gift does not exist today since there is no more need for it (claiming it to be an authenticity gift needed in the first century to give authority to the messenger of the Gospel). Others would say that it could exist today, but that they do not believe it does and that all that is claimed to be healing is not a genuine manifestation of the gift. Still others would claim that the gift does in fact exist today. There is ample evidence in Scripture from which to draw a definition and to give illustrations of this gift as it existed in New Testament times. One should note the double plurality (gifts of healings). It is not entirely clear to me what the double plurality emphasizes. The same kind of description occurs for several of the gifts (discernings of spirits, kinds of tongues, etc.). I will usually refer to this gift by the single word, healing. But keep in mind the double plurality idea.
definition	The gift of healing refers to the supernatural ability to heal people of physical diseases in response to a laying on of hands, or praying, or commanding to be healed or some combination of them by the person having the gift.
example	Acts 28:8 "And it came to pass that the father of Publius lay sick of a fever and of a bloody flux; to whom Paul entered in, and prayed, and laid his hands on him and healed him."
example	Acts 14:8-10 "And there sat a certain man at Lystra, impotent in his feet, being a cripple from his mother's womb, who never had walked: the same heard Paul speak: who steadfastly beholding him, and perceiving that he had faith to be healed, said with a loud voice, stand upright on thy feet. And he leaped and walked."
example	Acts 3:2,6,7,8 "And a certain man lame from his mother's womb was carried, who they laid daily at the gate of the temple which is called Beautiful, to ask alms of them that entered into the temple: Then Peter said, Silver and gold have I none; but such as I have give I thee: In the name of Jesus Christ of Nazareth rise up and walk. And he took him by the right hand, and lifted him up: and immediately his feet and ankle bones received strength. And he leaping up stood, and walked, and entered with them into the temple, walking, and leaping, and praising God."
N.T. function of gift	• Give authority to the message of those who exercised this gift (Acts 3, II Cor. 12:12, Heb. 2:4) • Humanitarian reasons (Acts 28:8)

HEALING (cont.)

---

comment	It seems that in the exercise of this gift that sometimes the recipient of the healing possessed "faith" to be healed (i.e. believed God could and would heal him). At other times the healing seemed to have <u>nothing</u> to do with the recipient and depended solely upon the person with the gift. And still other times it appears as if it depends totally upon God and not upon either the healer or the ones being healed. The phrase, the power of the Lord was present for healing, occurs several times in the Gospels. When the power of the Lord is present for healing the quality of faith in the one being healed and the quality of faith in the healer seemed to be overshadowed.

---

symptoms	• a desire to see God alleviate physical problems in people and the willingness to be used by God to do so. • an unusual ability to sense the power of God present for healing. • often comes in conjunction with the gift of word of knowledge. • the principle of contagion probably applies here. People who are around people who are seeing healing occur regularly, particularly with accompanying gifts involving word of knowledge, are very likely to sense that God is pointing out this gift in their lives.

---

caution	Whether or <u>not</u> this gift exists today is a question of its own apart from the definition of the gift. There does <u>not</u> seem to be exegetical evidence showing cessation of the gift. It would seem that the "authenticity" function giving authority to a presentation of the Gospel is still needed. Perhaps other means of authenticity do exist.

---

experience	Large numbers of Christians (pentecostals, neo-pentecostals) utilize this gift regularly in conjunction with their practice of Christianity.

MERCY synonym: showing mercy

introduction In general Christians should be tender-hearted and compassionate to those in need around them. But some Christians are endowed by God in a special way to sense and seek out and help those in need. The gift of mercy (showing mercy) is qualified with a descriptive phrase by Paul in Romans 12:8 which points out the attitude that should exist in one as he exercises this gift.

Greek basic word study On Mercy

	Etymological or literal rendering	English words	Central Idea
eleeo	related to basic word for compassion	obtain mercy have mercy have compassion have pity on show mercy receive mercy	in general to feel with the misery of another and to show sympathy by action

Related Words

eleeinos	miserable
elemon	merciful
elemosune	alms almsdeed
eleos	mercy

Synonym

oikteiro	to pity, to have compassion on

Qualifying Phrase

en hilaroteti	cheerfully, with a cheerful attitude

Related to

hilarotes	cheerfulness
hilaros	cheerful seen in II Cor. 9:8 Root of our English word hilarious

definition The gift of mercy refers to the capacity both to feel sympathy with those in need (especially those suffering and miserable) and to manifest this sympathy in some practical helpful way with a cheerful spirit so as to encourage and help those in need.

MERCY   (cont.)

---

example | Acts 9:36 "Now there was at Joppa a certain disciple named Tabitha, which by interpretation is called Dorcas: this woman was full of good works and almsdeeds (eleemosune, one of the related words) which she did."

---

modern day example | Amy Carmichael who served many years in India and saved countless young Indian girls from becoming temple prostitutes demonstrated over and over again the gift of mercy throughout her lifetime.

---

use |
- To practically express the love of God to people in need and thus prepare their hearts for acceptance of the Gospel message.
- To help alleviate problems of social concern as a part of the church's responsibility to society.

---

symptoms |
- Tears come easily as you hear or see things which sadden.
- Most people think of you as possessing a very empathetic personality.
- You want to reach out and help people in misery.
- You are unusually sensitive to the hurts of others.
- You have an unusual desire to express your love to helpless people.
- People in need like to have you around because you cheer them up.
- You are not easily repulsed by the sight of miserable people but instead you usually think, "How could I help?"

FEEDBACK ON NUMERICAL GIFTS

question Match the gifts below with their definitions or key words from definitions or uses or symptoms by placing the number of the gift in the blank beside the definition or key word or use or symptom.

1. apostleship   4. healing
2. evangelism   5. mercy
3. miracles   6. body evangelism

_____a. the primary means of God's reconciling men and women to Himself.

_____b. provides the context out of which the local church evangelism effectively reaches people.

_____c. having authority from God through a local church to begin new churches and establish them.

_____d. a miraculous intervention by God in a given situation for which God receives the recognition.

_____e. validates claims to the authenticity of the gospel message.

_____f. used to select, train, and appoint leadership for local churches.

_____g. a demonstration of corporate love, unity, Christian life-style, and concern for the community which authenticates the gospel message from a local church to its locale.

_____h. one symptom--the fact that people actually make discipleship commitments as a direct result or indirect result of your influence.

_____i. one symptom—you are not easily repulsed by the sight of miserable people but instead you usually think, "How could I help?"

_____j. the capacity both to feel sympathy with people in need to manifest this feeling through practical activity.

_____k. supernatural ability to heal people of physical disease.

answers

2 a.   6 b.   1 c.   3 d.   3,4 e.   1 f.
6 g.   2 h.   5 i.   5 j.   4 k.

GIFTS FOCUSED ON ORGANIC CHURCH GROWTH

introduction | Two gifts prove very necessary to the direction of the corporate life of a local church and to the enablement of this corporate life to be and to do what it should. The two gifts—helps and governments are described in the next part of this module.

2 gifts

GIFTS	PRIMARY THRUST IN LOCAL CHURCH
governments	help insure smooth operation of local church in terms of administrative functions
helps	enables the corporate life to function smoothly by doing support tasks which aid leaders and others

other leadership gifts—how related | The leadership gifts, apostleship, prophecy, teaching, pastoring, evangelism, (possibly ruling) also contribute to the organic growth of the church. However, they have strong focuses on maturity and numeric growth so were covered under those topics. The gifts of helps and governments are support leadership gifts which will help greatly in the organic growth of a church or other Christian structure. In my thinking I distinguish two groups of leadership gifts: directive and supportive. The directive gifts of apostleship, prophecy, teaching, pastoring, evangelism, (possibly ruling) will carry the main responsibility of seeking the Lord's direction for the groups for which these leadership gifts are responsible. The supportive gifts will primarily carry out the direction and enable the directive leaders to reach those goals God has given.

GOVERNMENTS   synonym: minister, administrative helps

| introduction | The word translated as governments occurs in the New Testament only in I Corinthians 12:28. A study of this word and its cognates which were used in the classic Greek of New Testament times indicated that the word has to do with guiding of affairs. It would seem natural to then say that it is one of the leadership gifts of the local church. However, it is listed in the Corinthians passage not with the leadership gifts, but with the supportive gifts. For this reason (and no other exegetical reason) I have chosen to identify this gift with the minister (function in Romans and I Peter) and assume it to be a supportive administrative gift which manages needed service functions in a local church rather than a leadership gift which guides the local church. The passage in Acts 6 would be an example of such a gift in action. |

background word study

	Greek	Etymological or literal rendering	English words	Central Idea
I Cor. 12:28	kubernesis	process of piloting	governments	to direct especially toward a goal
Related Words				
	kubernao	to steer or guide		to set the direction
	kuberthnetes	a steersman or pilot	shipmaster	the one having authority over the ship

| definition | The gift of governments involves a capacity to manage details of service functions within the church. |

| explanation | This supportive gift when exercised helps the church operate smoothly. As in the Acts 6 example it allows primary leadership gifts to focus their priorities. |

| example | Acts 6:1-4 presents a particular example of this concept. "And in those days when the number of disciples was multiplied, there arose a murmuring of the Grecians against the Hebrews, because their widows were neglected in the daily ministration. Then the twelve called the multitude of the disciples unto them and said, it is not fitting that we should leave the Word of God and serve tables. Wherefore, brethren, look ye out among you seven men of honest report full of the Holy Ghost and wisdom, whom we may appoint over this business. But we will give ourselves to prayer, and to the ministry of the word." |

GOVERNMENTS (cont.)

example (cont.)

> Here people were chosen in order to oversee the details and to
> support the widows in need and to free up the Apostles for
> service of the word. It was obviously considered of spiritual
> importance for high spiritual standards were placed upon those
> who were to serve.

symptoms

- You have a knack for organizing things.
- You like to standardize methods when doing something.
- You think in terms of helping others reach goals.
- You have a concern for the good of the whole group when you
  are in charge of a group.
- You like to do things which help others.
- You don't mind managing or carrying out the details involved
  in initial planning done by others.

HELPS

introduction	Where there are groups of people there are always practical needs. So it is with the church. And God has provided in his church people who have the abilities and the unselfish attitudes to serve and in very practical ways meet the temporal needs of others. Such is the nature of the gift of helps.

basic
word studies   TABLE OF WORDS RELATING TO CONCEPT OF GIFT OF HELPS

Basic Greek passage	Literal or etymological use	Translated by English word(s)	Central Thought
I Cor. 12:28 anti-lemphei	to take hold in front (i.e. to support)	helps	to serve aiding another (Abbot-Smith says plural of ministrations of deacons)

Related Words

	Abbot-Smith says antilempheis is used in classical Greek like bontheia
bontheia	a supportive strapping or bracing for a navy vessel etymologically came from two words meaning a shout and run=timely help and so used in Heb. 4:16
anti-lambanesthai	to take in turn, to aid, to assist, to help, in Acts 2:35 to support the weak
antechomai	to exercise a zealous care for as in I Thess. 5:14

definition	The gift of helps refers to the capacity to unselfishly meet the needs of others through practical service. Such service may be menial or domestic in nature.
comment	Normally one would fail to see that the gift of helps would require any special capacity. Especially is this the tendency since the nature of the Christian walk is to help others. However, this particular gift is included in a list of gifts and can therefore be assumed to be distinct from ordinary service that anyone can do. Perhaps too this is a distinctive gift because it contributes to spiritual growth.
symptoms	● A desire to help others. ● An ability to see ways that will help others.

HELPS (cont.)

_____

symptoms (cont.)

- An unselfish nature which likes to do tasks, menial, or otherwise which will help others.
- An ability to see temporal needs of others.
- A bent toward enjoying practical service more than theoretical service of conceptual nature.
- A willingness to do little jobs without any credit just for the joy of doing them and knowing they are a help to someone.
- Particularly in the church a willingness to do jobs which will allow the leadership gifts to be enhanced.

_____

uses

The gift of helps, is used:

- to render practical service in the church to needy church members.
- to do menial jobs of a practical nature which will free-up people to utilize leadership gifts.
- to help others reach their full potential.

_____

FEEDBACK ON ORGANIC GIFTS

question   Match the gifts below with their definition or key words from definitions or uses or symptoms by placing the number of the gift in the blank beside the definition or key word or use or symptom.

         1. governments   2. helps   3. neither governments or helps

_____a. The primary means of God's reconciling men and women to Himself.
_____b. One symptom—you are unusually sensitive to the hurts of others.
_____c. One symptom—you have a knack for organizing things.
_____d. One symptom—you don't mind managing details.
_____e. Capacity to unselfishly meet the needs of others through practical service.
_____f. One symptom—an ability to see ways that will help others.

answers   <u>3</u> a. <u>3</u> b. <u>1</u> c. <u>1</u> d. <u>2</u> e. <u>2</u> f.

FEEDBACK ON MODULE 2

---

questions

I. Match the kinds of growth indicated below with the gifts given below by placing the number of the growth in the blank beside the name of the gift.
    1. Maturity Church Growth
    2. Numerical Church Growth
    3. Organic Church Growth

_____a. evangelism	_____g. tongues	_____l. faith
_____b. healing	_____h. interpretation of	_____m. mercy
_____c. teaching	tongues	_____n. giving
_____d. exhortation	_____i. miracles	_____o. knowledge
_____e. governments	_____j. helps	_____p. discernment
_____f. apostleship	_____k. prophecy	_____q. pastoring
		_____r. wisdom

II. Fill in the name of a gift in the blank in the statements which follow the description and quotes below.

Description

A small group of less than 15 people from the First Presbyterian Church regularly meets on Wednesday evenings in the various homes of the members of the group (part of the church's decentralized efforts). The meetings begin around 7 PM and usually last for 2 hours or more. The group shares together concerning their needs, their weekly experiences, and their continuing discovery of Christ meeting their needs. They have developed an open relationship in which each member can honestly share the good and the bad because each knows the group really cares. The group also spends time in Bible study and discussion of how the things learned in Bible study can be put in practice. They usually close with a time of prayer—mostly conversational and usually participated in by everyone. Choruses or hymns frequently pop-up in the sharing time, or the Bible time, or the prayer time. The times together are warm. The members of the group consider it the highlight of each week. They make every effort to be at each group meeting. From the following comments see if you can ascertain some of the gifts that are used interdependently among the group.

A typical sampling of some of the group's conversation.

Mary said, "Jim, when you explain things like you did about that puzzling passage tonight, I really see what God means by it. I like the way you related it to the book as a whole."

John said, "Mary, that was a precious time of sharing. I don't see how you can work in that kitchen in the slum area and love those poor people so much. But I sure admire you and can see the love of Christ working through you."

(conversation continued on next page)

FEEDBACK ON MODULE 2 (cont.)

Jim said, "John when you shared how God had met your own heart's need through that verse in 2 Corinthians I can't tell you how encouraging it was to me. I've been going through a similar problem. God has sure used you to help me face it."

Martha, "I believe that God would have the kind of fellowship that we enjoy—such a vital Christianity—spread to our whole church. I have had a growing conviction about it and believe God is going to do a work of growth in love, unity, and in-depth fellowship in our church so that in a year's time our whole church will be alive like we are. I was reading again in John 17 just yesterday morning. I seem to be drawn back to this passage more and more lately. You know the prayer Christ prayed in verse 23. I believe he wants that kind of unity in our whole church and I am going to trust God for the answer to that prayer for our church. Oh how we need it."

Jerry said, "I made another friend at work today. In the most natural way I told him what has been happening in my life lately. He told me he wished he could know God that way. Not only that, but he invited me over to his house to explain it in detail. I can hardly wait. Just think next week this time he might know God like we do. Pray for me as I speak with him. If he comes to know Christ he can join Roy and me in our noontime Bible sharing (Roy made a decision to follow Christ two months ago as a result of Jerry's influence)."

If the kind of things described above recur frequently we could probably assume that,

    a. Mary has the gift of _____.
    b. Jim has the gift of _____.
    c. Martha has the gift of _____.
    d. John has the gift of _____.
    e. Jerry has the gift of _____.

III.   Match the gifts named below with passages (where more than one gift is indicated in a passage use the underlined prompt) listed below by placing the number of the gift in the blank beside the Scripture passage.

1. evangelism	7. tongues	12. faith
2. healing	8. interpretation	13. mercy
3. teaching	of tongues	14. giving
4. exhortation	9. miracles	15. knowledge
5. governments	10. helps	16. discernment
6. apostleship	11. prophecy	17. not clear which gift
		18. wisdom

_____a.   Rom. 12:8 "He that giveth, let him do it liberally."
_____b.   Titus 1:5 "For this cause I left thee in Crete, that thou shouldest set in order the things that are wanting and <u>ordain</u> elders in every city, as I had appointed thee."
_____c.   I Cor. 14:3 "But he that prophesieth speaketh unto men to ..."
_____d.   Acts 8:12 "But when they believed Philip's preaching the things concerning the Kingdom of God and the name of Jesus Christ, they were baptized, both men and women."

FEEDBACK ON MODULE 2 (cont.)

_____ e. Acts 18:26 "And he (Apollos) began to speak boldly in the synagogue, whom when Aquila and Priscilla had heard, they took him unto them and <u>expounded unto him the way of God more perfectly.</u>"

_____ f. I John 4:1 "Beloved believe not every spirit, <u>but test the spirits whether they are of God;</u> because many prophets are gone out into the world."

_____ g. Acts 9:36,39 "Now there was at Joppa a certain disciple named Tabitha, which by interpretation is called Dorcas: this woman was full of good works and <u>almsdeeds</u> which she did ... and all the widows stood by him (Peter) weeping and showing the coats, and garments which Dorcas made, while she was with them."

---

answers

I. <u>2</u> a. <u>2</u> b. <u>1</u> c. <u>1</u> d. <u>3</u> e. <u>2</u> f. <u>1</u> g. <u>1</u> h.

<u>2</u> i. <u>3</u> j. <u>1</u> k. <u>1</u> l. <u>2</u> m. <u>1</u> n. <u>1</u> o. <u>1</u> p.

<u>1</u> q. <u>1</u> r.

II. a. <u>mercy</u> b. <u>teaching</u> c. <u>faith</u> d. <u>exhortation (particularly the encouragement aspect)</u> e. <u>evangelism</u>

III. <u>14</u> a. <u>6</u> b. <u>11</u> c. <u>1</u> d. <u>3</u> e. <u>16</u> f. <u>13</u> g.

MODULE 3. ANALYZING YOURSELF SUBJECTIVELY

introduction | Paul says in Romans 12:3, "For I say through the grace given unto me, to everyone that is among you not to think of himself more highly than he ought to think; but to think soberly according as God hath dealt to every man the measure of faith." Or put in the vernacular, "You should have a correct evaluation of yourself." He then connects this idea to the different gifts God has given each member of the body. In other words we should evaluate ourselves in terms of God-given gifts. This module suggests several ways in which you can analyze yourself.

2 kinds of personal analyses | The kinds of helps toward personal analysis suggested in this module are:
- Personality Testing
- Inward Conviction Questionnaire

contents

objectives | By the time you complete this section,

- you will have an indication from the various subjective analyses of your spiritual gift(s).

cautions | None of these kinds of subjective analyses are conclusive in themselves (any one of them or all of them). Results of these tests are only suggestive at best. But taken in the context of this entire spiritual gifts unit they can certainly give strong pointers which you can use to aid you in confirming your gift through experience in your local church.

WHAT CAN BE LEARNED FROM PERSONALITY TESTS

introduction	Many kinds of personality tests are being used today to help people see themselves. No test is fool proof. But a good test when honestly reviewed with a trained counselor can be valuable to you not only in pointing out strengths and weaknesses in character traits, but in suggesting correlation between your traits and traits observed in people exercising certain spiritual gifts.
example	Taylor-Johnson Temperament Analysis Profile
where available	Psychological Publications Inc. 5300 Hollywood Blvd. Los Angeles, CA 90027
another example	The Predictive Index Organizational Survey, Personnel Appraisal
main use of testing	The main use of personality analysis tests is to allow a person to see himself and to see how he does see himself. Paul says we need to have an accurate self-appraisal; not too high nor too low. Tests help us approach this standard urged by Paul in Romans 12:3. In addition we may be able to develop strong traits and to overcome weak traits. Further, we may be able to correlate traits to a gift or gifts and in developing those traits be better able to exercise our gifts (see Gifts Correlated to Traits Table).
caution	The Scriptures do not explicitly give information concerning natural abilities and spiritual gifts. Sometimes God seems to use natural abilities in someone's spiritual gift. At other times a person's spiritual gift seems to be entirely different than you would have expected from analyzing their natural abilities. It may be that character traits may correlate just as well with spiritual gifts as natural abilities. That is, included in the spiritual gift may be inherent character traits which enhance the exercise of the gift.
related maps	see Gifts Correlated to Traits Table, 99

HOW TO USE THE GIFTS CORRELATED TO TRAITS TABLE

introduction   Please read the symptoms, traits, or descriptive phrases seen
in people having gifts for each of the gifts. Line through any
symptom, trait, or description which you think fits you. Count
the number you lined out for each gift and record it in the
column to the right of the gift (which says _____of some
number). If you have taken some personality test and reviewed
it with someone it will be much easier for you to know whether
the descriptions are really true of you or not. But even if
you have not go ahead and try this.

Step	Procedure	Example
1.	Read the Traits listed under the gift of apostleship.	strong self-image, strong sense of duty, willingness to take risks, creative and imaginative, tensive and impatient, confident drive to accomplish, objective, dominant, persistent, self-disciplined, very authoritative, more nervous than composed.
2.	Line out any phrases which you think fit you.	~~strong self image, strong sense of duty, willingness to take risks, creative and imaginative, tensive and impatient, confident drive to accomplish, objective, dominant, persistent, self-disciplined, very authoritative, more nervous than composed.~~
3.	Count the number of phrases you lined out and record in the column. I have_____of 12.	I have of these _6_ of 12
4.	Repeat procedures 1 - 3 above for each gift.	
5.	Record in the summary section (last page of traits table), 101, any gifts in which you have 1/2 or more of the traits. If you do not have any gifts with 1/2 or more then record the two gifts in which you have the most traits.	

GIFTS CORRELATED TO TRAITS TABLE

GIFTS	SOME SYMPTOMS, TRAITS, OR DESCRIPTIONS SEEN IN SOME PERSONS DEMONSTRATING THIS GIFT	I HAVE OF THESE
Apostleship	strong self-image, strong sense of duty, willingness to take risks, creative and imaginative, tensive and impatient, confident drive to accomplish, objective, dominant, persistent, self-disciplined, very authoritative, more nervous than composed	_____of 12
Prophecy	strong self-image, individualistic, strong sense of duty, does not particularly care what anybody thinks about what he does, probably a strong opinionated person, sometimes stubborn, willing to take an underdog role, more depressed than light-hearted about life and its problems, more expressive than inhibited, more dominant than submissive, more hostile than tolerant, more interested in own aims and desires than other people's	_____of 12
Evangelism	self-image varies but tends toward strong, individual who likes people, active socially, gets along well with others, more lighthearted than depressed, more expressive than inhibited, more sympathetic than indifferent, more subjective than objective, more tolerant of people than hostile toward them, more impulsive than self-disciplined, inclined to make decisions based on emotions	_____of 11
Governments	accurate self-image, skilled in detail, thorough and careful, makes decisions based strictly on facts and proven data, more interested in the welfare of group than own desires, more composed than nervous, more submissive than dominant, more objective than subjective	_____of 7
Helps	inclined toward low self-image, high sense of empathy, loyal, usually easy going, particularly interested in helping people, wants people to like him/her, congenial, very patient, listens to others uncritically, publicly more inhibited than expressive, more submissive than dominant, more tolerant of people than hostile to them, sincere person, good with mechanical service work	_____of 14

GIFTS CORRELATED TO TRAITS TABLE

Exhortation	inclined toward low self-image, empathetic, in a group more expressive than inhibited, responsive, more subjective than objective, more tolerant of people than hostile toward them, more impulsive than self-disciplined, more sympathetic than indifferent	____of 8
Word of Wisdom	accurate self-image, analytical, accumulator of knowledge, patient, more tolerant of people than hostile toward them, more objective than subjective, more composed than nervous, may or may not be active socially but when in a group people do pay attention when he says something, more conservative than radical	____of 9
Discernment	accurate self-image, will usually make decisions based on facts rather than emotions, probably a disciplinarian, accumulator of knowledge, serious minded, critical and analytical, may be introspective, logical step-by-step approach to things, tends more toward depression than light-heartedness, more indifferent than sympathetic, more objective than subjective, more hostile than tolerant, more self-disciplined than impulsive	____of 13
Faith	tends toward low self-image, usually optimistic, persistently clings to something, more subjective than objective, inclined to make decisions based on emotions rather than facts, willing to take risks impulsively, very loyal, introspective, more light-hearted than depressed, more sympathetic than indifferent, more impulsive than self-disciplined	____of 11
Giving	accurate self-image, more light-hearted than depressed, particularly interested in helping people, wants people to like him/her, accurate person, conscientious person, high sense of empathy, more sympathetic than indifferent	____of 8
Mercy	inclined toward low self-image, high sense of empathy, patient person, good natured, talks well with people and easy to talk to, wants people to like him, sincere, very responsive to people, more subjective than objective, inclined to make decisions based on emotions, tolerant of people, impulsive	____of 12

GIFTS CORRELATED TO TRAITS TABLE

Teaching	creative and imaginative, confident drive to accomplish, more objective than subjective, self-disciplined, authoritative when explaining things, makes decisions based on facts, tendency to talk more than listen, analytical, accumulator of knowledge, enjoys studying, likes to see things clearly, constantly analyzing better ways to say things or explain them, accurate self-image, sometimes strongly technically oriented, sometimes strongly methodical, intelligent, stimulates others to learn, enthusiastic when explaining something, people usually understand when he/she says things	_____of 19
Pastoring	authoritative in bearing, more dominant than submissive, high sense of empathy, more tolerant of people than hostile toward them, in a group more expressive than inhibited, more composed than nervous, people with needs are drawn to this person, able to resolve problems between people, tendency to compromise rather than go to either of two extremes, sensitive to hurt feelings or problems which cause loss of unity in a group	_____of 10

Summary

List here the gifts indicated by traits_____

_____

some problems with this analysis	• The traits describing the gift of exhortation have not proven as useful an indicator as other traits. Perhaps this is because the various aspects of exhortation can be expressed through many varying personality types. • People don't understand what the terms or phrases mean. • People misunderstand what I mean when I use some term or phrase because they may have learned it in another connection or context. • Some of the terms and phrases overlap in meaning--there needs to be a sharper distinction between terms. Or better yet some standard easily categorized list of traits (recognizable to all) should be used. I am hoping for outside help to do this for the next revision. • People with high self-image usually overrate themselves and indicate more gifts than they really have. • People with low images usually underrate themselves and indicate few or no gifts.
some ways to get around these problems	• Use the lists given here as "springboards" to discuss with others personality traits which you have which might be reflected in gifts. • Have others beside yourself take this analysis on you. Your analysis as compared and modified by someone else's analysis (who knows you well) will probably be a more accurate picture of you.

INWARD CONVICTION QUESTIONNAIRE FOR_____

introduction The inward conviction questionnaire seeks to gather information
which relates to five basic principles often seen in the way
that God leads people to identify and exercise their gifts.

- God honors your personal desires.
- A restless growing conviction to be involved in something
  may indicate that God will reveal a gift needed for the
  involvement.
- A God-directed specific call to a particular ministry
  indicates that you will have one or more gifts needed in
  that ministry.
- A forced situation may demand a certain gift or gifts to
  meet the situation. These gifts may already be there
  (latent) and will surface with the need or they may come
  spontaneously in answer to seeking them from God.
- Especially where leadership gifts are concerned, gifted
  leaders attract people who are potentially like-gifted.

The following questions should be answered with these basic
principles in mind. Perhaps God is speaking to you right now
in terms of one or more of these principles.

Fill out as many of the questions below as you can (i.e. those which really
apply to you). Then follow the directions on page 105 entitled HOW TO USE
THE INWARD CONVICTION QUESTIONNAIRE.

1. If I could do anything in the world that I wanted to (secular or
    spiritual) I would like to (describe in your own words what you would
    really like to do. In order to give absolute freedom to answer this
    question assume that whatever it is, it is in the perfect will of God for
    you to do it.)

2. Regardless of whether it is true that you possess them, check at least
    three gifts below that you would like to have in order of preference
    (1,2,3,):

_____prophecy	_____tongues	_____evangelism
_____teaching	_____interpretation of	_____miracles
_____knowledge	tongues	_____healing
_____pastoring	_____discernment	_____mercy
_____exhortation	_____faith	_____governments
_____giving	_____apostleship	_____helps
_____wisdom		

3. If you could have your choice of doing anything you wanted to using one
    or more of the gifts you checked in question two, what would you like to
    do? (Describe in your own words.)

INWARD questionnaire cont

4. In my past experience with God I have made the following promises or intents (maybe this was done as a result of a public committal or a private committal):

    Where or when committal done   Essence of inward intent or promise

    a.

    b.

    c.

5. I have had a growing restless conviction from within that,

    a. I should get involved in_____or

    b. there is a special need which I could help meet. (Describe it):

    c. To what gift would this conviction best relate?

    d. In what way?

6. I am certain that God has definitely called me to a specific ministry.

    a. How do you know you are certain about this call? Describe your call (when, where, or how or any circumstances relating to it):

    b. Describe the gift or gifts you feel are needed with this ministry.

    c. Which of these do you feel you best are fitted for?

7. I am in a situation at present (local church or other ministry) in which a certain gift or gifts are really needed. The situation demands this.

    a. Briefly describe the situation as you see it.

    b. name the gifts needed   why needed

    c. Can you see the gift(s) arising in any who are presently related to the situation? If so, who?

    d. Do you feel God could develop this gift in you (especially is this important if you don't see anyone else who might get this gift)?

        _____yes   _____no   _____unlikely   _____not sure

    e. Are you willing to be the channel for this needed gift?

        _____yes, definitely so   _____yes, if none of the others can

        _____would rather someone else have this gift

INWARD QUESTIONNAIRE (cont.)

8. Have you ever made (or even thought) the following statement (or equivalent statement) concerning the <u>ministry</u> of some Christian.

   a. I wish I could be like (<u>name of some Christian</u>)._____
   Even if I haven't there are one or more persons that I could make that statement about. _____   _____

   b. If so, describe what about the Christian (or Christians) or his ministry that prompted or could prompt you to make a statement.

   c. What ministry or strengths or spiritual gift(s) were demonstrated by the Christian(s) referred to in the statement.

9. Of the Christians I feel drawn to or respect for their contribution to God's work, the two I most respect have the following gift(s). (Use the number 1 for one of the Christians, use the number 2 for the other Christian--fill in the 1 or 2 beside any of the gifts listed below which the given Christian exercises):

_____prophecy	_____tongues	_____evangelism
_____teaching	_____interpretation of	_____miracles
_____knowledge	tongues	_____healing
_____pastoring	_____discernment	_____mercy
_____exhortation	_____faith	_____governments
_____giving	_____apostleship	_____helps
_____wisdom		

10. If I could be associated with a gifted Christian for special on-the-job training in terms of the gift that he or she uses,

    a. I would choose,

       I. (Name some individual)_____

       II. Somebody having a ministry (describe the ministry):

       III. _____I don't know anyone or any ministry which fits me.

    b. If you chose a particular person,

       I. Why would you choose that person?

       II. What particular strengths, or abilities, or spiritual gifts does that person have?

HOW TO USE THE INWARD CONVICTION QUESTIONNAIRE

introduction	Assuming you have filled out all the answers you can on the questionnaire you are now ready to draw some possible conclusions from your answers

STEP	PROCEDURE
1.	Fill in the chart below by examining your answers to the questions indicated.
2.	After filling in the entire chart, put any gifts which occurred two or more times on the chart beside the Summary of Findings line below the chart.

CHART EXPRESSING POSSIBLE GIFTS IN TERMS OF INWARD CONVICTIONS

Principle Involved	Use your answers to	And list here any gifts which could be reflected in your answers
GOD HONORS PERSONAL DESIRES	Questions 1,2,3,4	
A RESTLESS GROWING CONVICTION MAY INDICATE A GIFT	Question 5	
A GOD-DIRECTED CALL TO A SPECIFIC TASK ENTAILS A GIFT OR GIFTS NEEDED IN IT	Question 6	
MY SITUATION DEMANDS A GIFT(S) IN ORDER FOR IT TO PROSPER AS GOD WANTS IT TO	Question 7	
GIFTED LEADERS ATTRACT PEOPLE WHO WILL LATER EXERCISE THE SAME GIFTS SEEN IN THE LEADERS	Question 8,9,10	

SUMMARY OF FINDINGS:_____

MODULE 4.   CONFIRMING YOUR GIFT THROUGH OTHERS
_____

introduction   What do other Christians think your spiritual gift is?
Especially those with whom you have close association? It is in
the context of use and ministry (especially mutual ministry)
that gifts emerge.   A sit-and-soak Sunday Christian will
probably never know his spiritual gift(s) nor will others. If
you have been involved in a church where freedom to exercise
gifts is not only permitted, but actively encouraged, then
others of your fellowship will most likely be able to see your
gift(s), sometimes even when you can't. The form to be used
with others will prove extremely useful only in a church which
at least has some interdependent body activity.
_____

contents
of
Module 4

_____

reminder   After you have the information completed in the forms, don't
forget to mark off your progress on the checklist on page 35.
_____

HOW TO USE THE FORM FOR OUTSIDE CONFIRMATION

introduction   Use the procedure below to determine how best to use the form for outside confirmation.

Step	Procedure	
	IF	THEN
1.	You have not had much church related experience, OR your church does not meet many of the conditions listed on p. 108 (CONDITIONS UNDER WHICH OUTSIDE CONFIRMATION PROVES USEFUL) OR No one in your church really knows that much about you.	Don't give out the form. Begin now to have an active vital participation in a local church. Plan on using the form in the future.
2.	Your experience is related more to Christian work other than direct church ministry.	Skip to step 6.
3.	Your church does not hold the doctrine of spiritual gifts or by using the form you might cause controversy.	Don't use the form. Trust God to give outside confirmation some other way.
4.	You have been active in a church where at least one or more of the conditions listed on p. 108 and there is a plurality of leadership.	Give a copy of the form to two leaders preferably those having apostleship, or discernment, or teaching gifts. Also give a copy of the form to two close friends preferably those who have participated with you in a ministry group.
5.	You have been active in a church which does not have a plurality of leaders.	Give one form to the pastor or recognized leader. Give two forms to close friends.
6.	You have been active in Christian work other than direct church functions (e.g. small groups, other Christian organizations).	Get one or two people who have been involved with you to fill out the forms.
7.	It is possible, after the forms have been filled out,	Talk with the people who filled out the forms, discussing their answers and seeking their advice about using your gifts.

CONDITIONS UNDER WHICH OUTSIDE CONFIRMATION PROVES USEFUL

---

things
which
contribute
to outside
confirmation

If one or more of the following occurs in your local church (or other Christian experience) then use of the form may prove helpful. If a number of them occur then by all means use the form.

- A body-life ministry is practiced by the church.

- The church has a dispersed church mentality as well as a gathered church mentality.

- There are a number of small group activities in which members help each other grow.

- There is a plurality of leaders with complementary gifts directing the organic growth of the church.

- Gifts are taught in the church.

- Members are not only free to use their gift(s) but are strongly exhorted to do so. In fact, there is training along gift-oriented lines.

- The reciprocity commands (...one another commands) are a norm for the church.

- Members participate vitally not superficially in the gathered church functions of prayer, teaching, worship, sharing, and discipline.

FORM FOR OUTSIDE CONFIRMATION OF SPIRITUAL GIFTS OF_____

Filled out by_____(circle one) leader in church
                                                        friend
                                                        other (explain)

The following list of gifts will be referred to in the questions below.
Please see definitions on the following pages for the sense in which these
words are used.

_____prophecy   _____interpretation   _____evangelism
_____teaching   of tongues   _____miracles
_____knowledge   _____discernment   _____healing
_____pastoring   _____faith   _____mercy
_____exhortation   _____giving   _____governments
_____tongues   _____apostleship   _____helps
_____wisdom

Use your background knowledge and experience with the person named above to
answer the following.

1. Mark with a C any gift listed above which you are definitely **Certain** the
    person has.

2. Mark with a P any gift listed above which you think might be a **Potential**
    gift in the person.

3. Mark with an F any gift above which you have actually observed the person
    using **Fruitfully**.

4. For each gift you marked with a C (certain), tell why you feel it to be a
    gift.

5. For each gift you marked as P (potential), tell why you feel it to be
    a potential gift.

6. For each gift you marked F (fruitfully), illustrate what you meant.

7. Which gift that you have marked above do you feel should be the priority
    gift used by this person? Why?

8. Would you advise how this person could train or better use this gift in
    the church?

9. Would you mark with an O (own) your gift(s)?

SUMMARY DEFINITIONS--SPIRITUAL GIFTS

PROPHECY--The gift of prophecy is the capacity to deliver publicly truth (of a predictive nature as well as a situational word) from God in order to exhort, edify, or console believers and to convince non-believers of God's truth.

TEACHING--A person who has the gift of teaching is one who has the ability to instruct, explain, or expose Biblical truth in such a way as to cause believers of a church to understand the Biblical truth and to acquire the truth for their own use.

KNOWLEDGE--The gift, word of knowledge, represents the capacity to receive supernaturally revealed knowledge which otherwise could not or would not be known.

WISDOM--The gift, word of wisdom, represents the capacity to know the mind of the Spirit in a given situation and to communicate clearly the situation, facts, truth, or application of facts and truth to meet the need of the situation.

EXHORTATION--the gift of exhortation is the capacity to urge people to action in terms of applying Scriptural truth, or to encourage people generally with Scriptural truth, or to comfort people through application of Scriptural truths to their needs.

TONGUES--The gift of tongues is an ability given spontaneously by the Holy Spirit to an individual to speak in a language unknown to the speaker.

INTERPRETATION OF TONGUES--The gift, interpretation of tongues, is a gift whereby a believer is given an ability spontaneously by the Holy Spirit to translate the utterances of one using the gift of tongues.

DISCERNMENT--The gift of discernment is the analytical capacity to distinguish truth from non-truth by judging the truth or non-truth in terms of revealed truth or principles taken from that truth. Inherent in this gift is the ability to discern the spirit or spirits which are behind the situation. In its widest sense it is the judgment between right and wrong.

FAITH--The gift of faith is that unusual capacity to recognize in a given situation that which God intends to do generally and to trust Him for it until He brings it to pass. It is most likely expressed through prayer with God (i.e. the prayer of faith) though it may simply be a belief in a vision of what God can and will do in some situation.

GIVING--The gift of giving is the capacity to give liberally to meet the needs of others and yet to do so with a purity of motive which senses that the giving is a simple sharing of that which God has provided.

APOSTLESHIP--The gift of apostleship pertains to one who has been selected as a representative of a local church having authority from God through them and under authority to them for the purpose of beginning new churches and establishing and confirming leadership in these new churches. This gift would also apply to one who has authority from God to begin new mission structures.

SUMMARY DEFINITIONS--SPIRITUAL GIFTS cont

EVANGELISM--The gift of evangelism in general refers to the capacity to challenge people publicly and privately through various communicative methods with the message of salvation in Christ so as to see them respond by taking initial steps in Christian discipleship.

MIRACLES--The gift, working of miracles, is a gift in which the person exercising the gift invokes the miraculous intervention of God to a given situation with the result that God receives recognition for the supernatural intervention.

HEALING--The gift of healing refers to the supernatural ability to heal people of physical diseases in response to a laying on of hands, or praying, or commanding to be healed or some combination of them by the person having the gift.

MERCY--The gift of mercy refers to the capacity both to feel sympathy with those in need (especially those suffering and miserable) and to manifest this sympathy in some practical helpful way with a cheerful spirit so as to encourage and help those in need.

GOVERNMENTS--The gift of government involves a capacity to manage details of service functions within the local church or mission structures.

HELPS--The gift of helps refers to the capacity to unselfishly meet the needs of others through practical service. Such service may be menial or domestic in nature.

PASTORING--The pastoral gift is the capacity to exercise influence over a group so as to lead it toward a goal or purpose with particular emphasis on the capacity to make decisions for, to protect from error, and to disseminate truth primarily by modelling for the purpose of maturing the group toward Christlikeness.

MODULE 5. CONFIRMING YOUR GIFT THROUGH EXPERIENCE

introduction God has given us gifts so that we can serve the church and bring forth results which are pleasing to Him. It is primarily through <u>use</u> which brings <u>results</u> that we and others in our church recognize gifts. So, if you think you have some gift and perhaps others agree with you, then check your experience. Does it confirm your thinking? This module gives an experience questionnaire which forces you to think back over your Christian experience and activities to help you confirm the activities and experience in relationship to gifts.

contents of   <u>Description</u>   <u>page</u>
Module 5

reminder   After you have completed the experience questionnaire don't forget to mark off your progress on the checklist on page 35. Also make certain you fill out the Summary of Findings page 121. The Summary of Findings page allows you, on one page, to compare all that you have found out about your spiritual gift(s).

HOW TO USE THE EXPERIENCE QUESTIONNAIRE

Step	Procedure
1.	Recognize that the statements given are <u>not</u> all the statements which could be given. Hopefully they are representative. Perhaps a statement as given does not exactly fit you but by changing it slightly it would be true for you. Feel free to credit yourself with a modified statement or even substitute statement implying the same kind of outward expression of some gift.
2.	Place a checkmark beside each statement which you feel is true to your experience. Don't mark the ones you wish were true but aren't.
3.	Note that the questions are grouped according to gifts. Questions Gifts 1 - 6 apostleship 7 - 21 evangelism 22 - 34 mercy 35 - 44 prophecy 45 - 58 teaching 59 - 62 word of knowledge 63 - 70 word of wisdom 71 - 82 exhortation 83 - 93 discernment 94 - 101 faith 102 - 108 giving 109 - 116 governments 117 - 124 helps 125 - 134 pastoring
4.	Note below the number of questions you marked in each category. _____of 6 on apostleship _____of 15 on evangelism _____of 13 on mercy _____of 10 on prophecy _____of 14 on teaching _____of 4 on word of knowledge _____of 8 on word of wisdom _____of 12 on exhortation _____of 11 on discernment _____of 8 on giving _____of 7 on governments _____of 8 on faith _____of 8 on helps _____of 10 on pastoring
5.	List under summary any gifts on which you scored 1/2 or more of the questions or if you didn't have any gifts with 1/2 or more then list the 2 gifts with highest percentage of questions checked. SUMMARY (1)_____ (2)_____ (3)_____ (4)_____

EXPERIENCE QUESTIONNAIRE

| instructions | Read through the How to Use the Experience Questionnaire for specific instructions on using the Experience Questionnaire. Place a checkmark beside each statement which is true for you. |

___1. I instigated the movement to begin a new church.

___2. I started a new church which exists today.

___3. I am a charter member of a church.

___4. I am certain that God has called me to do church planting.

___5. I have been involved in selecting leaders for church work.

___6. I have been commissioned or ordained or licensed or have otherwise been authoritatively recognized for a full-time gospel ministry.

___7. I have been influential in a number of people becoming Christians and later church members.

___8. I have done door-to-door "cold-turkey" witnessing and have seen some make decisions.

___9. I have witnessed on my job with the result that several people are now Christians who would not be so if I hadn't helped them along.

___10. I have helped set up an evangelistic thrust requiring serious planning.

___11. I have taken part in an evangelistic thrust in which I individually challenged people with the salvation message and saw positive results.

___12. I have had freedom to turn natural conversations with individuals into witnessing situations and have seen individuals come to Christ.

___13. I have invited people to various evangelistic activities several times and have seen several come to Christ.

___14. I have shared my testimony at a public evangelistic thrust with the result that my participation helped bring about positive results.

___15. I have prayed specifically for several lost people by name and have seen them come to Christ.

___16. I have been the main speaker at public evangelistic meetings and have seen people come to Christ.

___17. I have participated in a small group which met regularly and was used by God to influence many to come to Christ.

___18. I have used tracts or booklets with many people and have seen several come to Christ.

___19. I have written letters to people in which I witnessed to them and have seen positive results through this letter writing.

___20. I have used some plan for presenting Christ to individuals such as the Roman Road, the Bridge, the 4 Spiritual Laws or like technique and have seen a number of people make actual committals to discipleship.

___21. I have shared my conversion testimony or other present testimony about God's working in my life with many individuals.

___22. I have been involved in a social outreach program in a large city which sought to help needy people.

___23. I have helped down-and-outers through some church related program.

___24. I have helped physically handicapped people; I cheer them up.

___25. I have been involved in a literacy program or other educational program to help underprivileged children or adults.

___26. I have taken food baskets to poor people.

___27. I have helped distribute clothing to needy people.

EXPERIENCE QUESTIONNAIRE (cont.)

____28. I have ministered to people through some medical activity and know that my ministry done cheerfully has helped others.

____29. I have contributed financially to programs helping orphans or other underprivileged.

____30. I have served as a houseparent (or other equivalent worker) in some orphanage program.

____31. I have worked on a regular basis with alcoholics and become empathetically involved with them, and helped several to recover.

____32. I have been involved in a prison rehabilitation program and know my cheerful influence has helped some.

____33. I have been involved so as to practically help drug addicts.

____34. I have helped unwed mothers face their problems and seen some of them straighten up their lives as a result of my help.

____35. I have been asked by my church to speak publicly to the church on a given issue of importance to the church.

____36. I have shared my testimony before a large church or other group and know that God used it to move people.

____37. I have spoken before groups containing believers and unbelievers and have given messages (not evangelistically oriented) which have caused unbelievers to assert the truth of what I said and to recognize God for who He is.

____38. I have more than once become convinced that God was giving me a message to meet a given situation and I have given that message authoritatively to the group concerned with the result that they were moved by God.

____39. I have experienced that when I speak most people listen and there is a definite dichotomy of response: some definitely for and some definitely against what I have said.

____40. I have been compelled when in a group in which discussion was taking place to interrupt and give an impassioned speech taking a definite stand on some issue. Often I have felt that God pressed me to speak.

____41. I find that when speaking publicly I often speak with deep emotional tones which God uses to break hearts so that there is a hearing to my message.

____42. I have felt that God has given me a word concerning some future event or some word telling my church or group what to do in the future.

____43. It has happened several times to me that when I spoke to a group (even though I didn't know their needs) that many have commented to me afterwards that what I said must have been from God because it dealt perfectly with a situation in the group.

____44. It has been my repeated experience to admonish a group when I know there is something wrong because I want to face the situation rather than let it ride.

____45. I have taught regularly in a Sunday School class and know my teaching has changed several lives.

____46. I have taught regularly in a small group situation and can definitely point out several people who have applied my teaching to their lives.

____47. I have read the Bible through a number of times.

EXPERIENCE QUESTIONNAIRE (cont.)

___48. I have made a special study of Jesus' parables to gain principles to use when I taught.

___49. I have used the lecture method with such success that I can maintain attention spans of groups for 50 or more minutes.

___50. I have led discussion groups so that people discover truth for themselves and apply it to their lives.

___51. I have taught a Bible Conference to a group.

___52. I have planned my teaching period to accomplish measured objectives and have evaluated these periods for effectiveness.

___53. It has been my experience that I can usually hear a question, interpret it correctly, and give an answer which gives information which explains the point of the question.

___54. I have been called upon by various groups outside my own church to teach various subjects to them.

___55. I have repeatedly received comments after some class in which I participated to the effect that my contribution sure helped clarify and explain points in the discussion.

___56. I have made it a point to study educational books or magazines and communication books or magazines in order to sharpen my own skills in communication.

___57. I have tried some unusual things or methods in order to communicate effectively. Some have really failed while others have really succeeded.

___58. It has become habitual for me to seek feedback whenever I am communicating to a group in order to know what has been learned and what I must do to correct my communication in the future.

___59. I have several times had strong impressions when in a group meeting of some idea that related to the group. The idea related to something that I would not have known had not God given it to me.

___60. Sometimes I see pictures in my mind of something that I feel God wants me to communicate to a group.

___61. In healing situations I often seem to know, spontaneously, that someone has a certain kind of health problem that God wants to heal.

___62. I have suddenly known things that are needed by the group--though I didn't know how I came to know them.

___63. I have studied Job, Psalms, and Proverbs to the extent that it is almost second nature for me to transfer principles seen in them to life situations.

___64. It has often been my experience in group situations that I could clearly , though admittedly intuitively, see what must be done and was able to communicate this to the group by applying correct Scriptural principles to the situation.

___65. I have often had individuals ask me for my opinion concerning some situation they faced and amazing as it may seem some Scriptural phrase or passage or other "advice" came to mind which I was able to convey to them convincingly so that they saw it as a word from God for their problem.

___66. I have often been convinced in my own mind that the Holy Spirit has given me an answer and led me in my choice of words in order that what I said would be received well.

EXPERIENCE QUESTIONNAIRE (cont.)

____67. People have often remarked to me that they have taken some comment that I made as a word from God to them concerning some issue or decision they must make.

____68. Many times I have thought the following (or equivalent), "It is clear how God sees this thing; why don't these people see things God's way?"

____69. I have received deep satisfaction when people have applied my advice to their situations and later received clear confirmation that the advice was God-given.

____70. It is easy for me to match some current situation with a Biblical character or historical event in Bible times and draw out some application for the current situation.

____71. I have often corrected another believer by showing him his error and giving him a Scriptural principle to help him with the result that the correction was applied to life.

____72. I have written letters from time-to-time to friends in which there were comments which proved to be very encouraging to these friends.

____73. I have found it my experience that I am easy to talk to and often have people share with me heart-to-heart talk.

____74. In small groups with which I have been associated it is not uncommon for someone to tell me that something I said has been a real comfort to them.

____75. I often am the one to urge the group to action especially when they are bogged down and indecisive on some issue.

____76. People often look to me to console someone who is facing a hard time.

____77. I find it my experience that I am very sensitive to people and can recognize that they are hurting though others in contact with these people never know they are hurting.

____78. I try to go out of my way to give a cheerful word to people around me and find that I usually encourage people in a general way.

____79. Many times things I say, whether to groups or individuals, cause people to become convicted.

____80. I know for certain that a number of things have happened in individual's lives and in my church situation in general because I have given a Scriptural admonition which was heeded.

____81. I often counsel with people.

____82. I have read a number of books dealing with psychology on a popular level in order that I might better understand people and be able to talk with them in a way to help them.

____83. I have often been able to recall many passages throughout the Bible which in some way relate to some given topic.

____84. It is almost second nature for me to analyze what a person says to see if it matches what I think Scripture teaches.

____85. People have often remarked to me that I have a way of cutting through all the cobwebs and getting to the real issue.

____86. I have a number of times corrected comments where they disagree with the tenor of Scripture with the result that the modified truth was accepted by all.

____87. It has been my repeated experience for people to ask me a question similar to the following, "Is it really true what he said?"

EXPERIENCE QUESTIONNAIRE (cont.)

___88. Though I don't always comment on it, I am bothered by much public ministry because I notice very quickly when preachers or teachers misinterpret or misapply Scriptural truth. It doesn't seem to bother others.

___89. I often catch myself not paying attention to some conversation because I have become interested in analyzing in detail something spoken in the conversation.

___90. I am often the one who has to bring it to the attention of others that a particular practice is inconsistent with some Scriptural imperative.

___91. I often catch subtle errors in religious books which if not caught could cause real trouble with believers.

___92. Upon occasion I recognize that in a situation I am being confronted by a spirit power and I am able to sense what kind of spirit is involved.

___93. Though I do seem to have a critical bent and am misunderstood by some people I know for certain that a number of issues on which I have given modified or different views have turned out to be correct and have helped our church avoid pitfalls.

___94. I have often prayed the "prayer of faith". God has answered many of these prayers. He will answer the rest.

___95. A number of times in my personal Bible reading times I have been convinced that God would have me claim certain promises for certain given situations. I have done this and have seen many of these promises fulfilled.

___96. Most of my prayers are specific because I want to know when the answer comes.

___97. People often come to me and ask me to pray for some situation because they feel my prayers get answered.

___98. I have read many times the Old Testament accounts which picture God doing miraculous things for his people. These passages have encouraged me to trust God in tough situations that my church has faced. God did it for them and He can meet us too.

___99. When problems arise my natural inclination is to trust God to somehow meet it while most in my church first try to analyze the problem or seek some way to solve it.

___100. There have been times when I have a conviction that I am sure is from God. I recognized that what God wanted done would require a "risk" in faith. In those times I learned to trust God to do those things. Our whole group has been encouraged to trust God more because of my example of stepping out in faith.

___101. It is not my nature to brag about my various exercises of faith and many of them are unknown to people, but even so, I am certain that God has used some of my experiences of trusting in unusual ways to encourage others to believe and pray with expectancy.

___102. I have at times given to help others with money that I needed. Some would probably think that foolish if they knew.

___103. I have been able to do without things (to me they are luxuries anyway) that others consider necessary in order to give more to God's work.

___104. God somehow seems to bring to my attention financial needs of people in my church (many times unintentional ways). I have given to people like this. Few know about some of these gifts.

EXPERIENCE QUESTIONNAIRE (cont.)

___105. I have consistently given more than 1/3 of my income to God's work.

___106. There have been times when I sensed some special financial need but did not have the finances to meet it. And then money came in some non-normal way. I knew that God wanted me to meet the need. So I gave.

___107. I have an inward joy in giving to meet a need. And it doesn't make any difference to me whether anyone ever knows about it or not.

___108. I am certain that God has given me special abilities to make money. I know that this is because he expects to use me as a channel to give large amounts to his cause.

___109. I presently serve as a deacon(ess) of my church.

___110. I have served as a church clerk or treasurer or other such position.

___111. I have served as a Sunday School Superintendent or other such position requiring my organizational ability.

___112. I have overseen the church property in some supervisory responsibility.

___113. I have been in charge of distributing benevolence funds in several church projects to needy people.

___114. I have been chosen on several committees which were formed to solve some administrative problems in conjunction with our church programs.

___115. I often am asked to arrange for the details of meetings, making sure everything is ready.

___116. I have been placed in charge of several programs (like VBS, Awana, etc.) which require organizational ability.

___117. I am very skillful with my hands and enjoy doing maintenance jobs on church property.

___118. I can fix almost anything and have gladly used my skill to help church members who needed my help.

___119. I have helped a number of people in my church with practical things even though it meant I put off something I needed to do for myself.

___120. I don't mind doing some task, menial or not, if I know it will free some other church member to exercise his gift.

___121. I have often been one of the first to volunteer for something the pastor felt was needed concerning the church.

___122. I don't mind unexpected guests in the home if I know we are helping them.

___123. Several times the pastor or someone else in the church has asked me to help accommodate guests. I gladly accepted the call.

___124. I find real satisfaction in doing practical things that will help others and try to seek opportunities to do so joyfully.

___125. I am presently serving as a pastor of a church.

___126. I am presently serving as a member of the leadership group of my church.

___127. I am presently responsible for the spiritual welfare of a group of people.

___128. In my past experience on the controlling group of our church I have been able to avert crises situations because I thought through possible consequences of decisions and was able to choose the best decision.

___129. My example in Christian living has had a decided impact on the group for whom I feel spiritually responsible.

EXPERIENCE QUESTIONNAIRE (cont.)

___130. In my church group I am often called upon to listen to people's problems because my counsel is generally well-balanced and good for the group as a whole.
___131. I have personally discipled several people of the group I am responsible for so that their progress toward maturity is evident.
___132. I am considered by a number of people in my church as a spiritual leader.
___133. I have repeatedly motivated groups of people toward goals or to carry out plans which I originated.
___134. I am one of the people most concerned with the spiritual progress of my church and by virtue of my influence will be able to do something about it.

HOW TO USE THE SUMMARY OF FINDINGS

Step	Procedure
1.	Fill in each column of the Summary of Findings chart by referring to the indicated pages for the various means of indicating your gift.
2.	List under "I should try to develop" column any gifts which seemed to be corroborated in several of the columns.
3.	Use the list under the "I should try to develop" and focus your study of Section III on these gifts.

SUMMARY OF FINDINGS

Indications of Possible Gifts From			
Gifts Correlated to Traits Table see page 99	Inward Conviction Questionnaire see page 102	Outside Confirmation see page 111	Experience Questionnaire see page 116

I should try to develop

HOW TO DEVELOP YOUR GIFT

PREVIEW: SECTION III.   HOW TO DEVELOP YOUR GIFT

introduction   Section I gave some overall considerations concerning spiritual
               gifts.   It concluded by suggesting a fourfold procedure to
               insure that you would profit from teaching on spiritual gifts.

                    1.   Identify your gift.
                    2.   Set out a plan to develop your gift.
                    3.   Choose your service in terms of your gift.
                    4.   Use your gift.

               Section II then dealt with the first procedure—Identify Your
               Gift—and gave detailed help for identifying your gift.   You
               should have tentatively identified your gift(s) by the time you
               get to the present section. And you should be anxious for some
               suggestions for developing it.   Section III will give some
               suggestions for procedures 2,3, and 4 listed above.

contents   <u>Description</u>   <u>page</u>
section III

objectives   By the time you finish this section you should have listed
               several suggestions you intend to follow for developing your
               gift over the short range and should have listed a possible
               guideline for long-term training of your gift.   In addition you
               should list several activities which allow you to use your gift.

SOME PRELIMINARIES

introduction	This section seeks to suggest some practical guidelines for developing some of the gifts. These suggestions are <u>not</u> given "ex cathedra". Some may prove useful, others may <u>not</u>. The main idea underlying these suggestions is simply this, "Find practical ways to develop skills or abilities which are used in the exercise of your gifts".
pre-suppositions	Several pre-suppositions should be understood before studying this section.

- For you to take steps to develop your gift is <u>not</u> incompatable with dependence upon the Holy Spirit. All of the suggestions given herein presuppose that you are trusting the Holy Spirit concerning your gift and in terms of his sanctifying presence in your life. That is, an unwritten first procedure for developing any gift is,

  TRUST THE HOLY SPIRIT TO LEAD YOU AND TO BRING
  TO MIND HIS PLANS FOR DEVELOPING YOUR GIFT.

- You consider the exercise of your gift(s) the most important ministry you will contribute in your lifetime. Therefore, the development of it and use of it will be given top priority in life time goal setting.

- These suggestions are not vocation centered. Apart from use of leadership gifts at regional level, use of most of the gifts does <u>not</u> necessitate a full-time Christian occupation (though concentrated development and use of some of the gifts are enhanced by a full-time Christian vocation).

- The suggestions are use-oriented. They require hard work. Most of the developmental suggestions require long term planning and discipline to carry out. However, they will insure that you use your gift most productively.

caution	Don't be discouraged when you read some of the overwhelming procedures—especially those dealing with mastery of the Bible. Remember, over a life-time, done little-by-little, they can be accomplished.
note	I am not sure how to suggest the development of some gifts. For many of the gifts thoughts come readily to mind. For those with no specifically-given ideas, there is a major procedure. Find people who are using the gift you are interested in developing. Spend time with them in an "informal apprenticeship." That is, watch them as they use their gift. You will learn more in "on-the-job" experiential learning than in most any other method. I particularly suggest this as a major method for developing the gifts: healing, mercy, miracles (particularly those activities involving power over the spirit world), governments.

HOW TO DEVELOP THE GIFT OF PROPHECY

introduction	Some skills or other features in the forth-telling aspect of the gift of prophecy can be developed. The predictive aspect (if extant) is not developable but comes directly from God. The authoritative, forceful manner inherent in the prophetical public ministry is less developed than inherited. However, the ability to move people publicly can be developed. One can certainly build up a Scriptural background and an awareness of current happenings in order to be sensitive to God's word for a given situation. The following suggestions, then, hint at ways to prepare one with a prophetical gift to be alert for God's word through him. Many of these suggestions are life-time procedures. They will not be accomplished overnight. The prophetical gift, well-developed, will be used in the regional church as well as the local church in taking a stand on the issues of our day. This is certainly needed.

G I V E N	You wish to prepare yourself for God to use your prophetical gift.

STEP	PROCEDURE	PROCEDURAL FOLLOW-UP SUGGESTIONS
1.	YOU MUST SEEK TO HAVE A COMPREHENSIVE GRASP OF THE ENTIRE SCOPE OF SCRIPTURE.	1. See teaching procedures 1,2 p. 130,131. 2. You must be immersed in the Scriptures at all times. 3. Particularly must you be able to tie the Bible together and see God's purposes and plans as they are revealed through Scripture.
2.	SPEND A MAJOR PORTION OF YOUR STUDY TIME MASTERING THE PREDIC-TIVE PASSAGES.	1. See Chart of Passages Apt For Study With Prophetical Gift, p. 129 2. Master the hermeneutical principles for prophecy, symbols, figurative language, and poetical language since much of pre-dictive literature uses these. 3. Set up a schedule to study the predictive books and passages which progresses from less difficult to more difficult passages. 4. Read extra-Biblical books; many are available today on prophecy.

HOW TO DEVELOP THE GIFT OF PROPHECY (cont.)

STEP	PROCEDURE	PROCEDURAL FOLLOW-UP SUGGESTIONS
3.	BE VERY CONSISTENT IN APPLYING TRUTH TO YOUR OWN LIFE.	1. Part of a public authoritative image comes from a rugged "uncompromising-with-truth" life-style. 2. Discipline yourself to specifically apply Scripture. Write down your applications specifically. Review them periodically.
4.	DEVELOP EXHORTIVE SKILLS.	1. See procedures 1,4 under Developing the Gift of Exhortation which deal primarily with admonition (see page 137). 2. Other exhortation procedures may prove helpful.
5.	STUDY CURRENT TRENDS.	1. Keep abreast of world news situations especially as they relate to God's intents in the Scriptures. 2. Study current trends in practical ecclesiology. Seek to interpret the movements and their significance. 3. Use questions to prod your thinking: How do these events or movements relate to revealed truth? Are there subtle traps we should be aware of in our group? What is God seeking to show us through these movements?
6.	DEVELOP SKILLS OF RHETORIC FOR MASS COMMUNICATIONS.	1. Read good books on rhetoric. 2. Seek to transfer principles to your own life-style. 3. Be alert for illustrations which move. 4. Learn to speak to affect the emotional and volitional realms. 5. Read practical books on communications (see Words On Target, Nichols). 6. Use homiletical principles which deal with application or persuasion.
7.	BE ESPECIALLY ALERT FOR CRISES SITUATIONS.	1. The nature of your gift is such that God will use you to meet unusual situations both in the local and regional churches. 2. Ask God to give you his Word for these situations. 3. Use opportunities to speak in the gathered church and regional church, especially where God has given insight.

Related Maps see PROPHECY, p. 52, ...PASSAGES FOR STUDY WITH PROPHETICAL GIFT, p.129

CHART OF PASSAGES APT FOR STUDY WITH PROPHETICAL GIFT

PASSAGES	OBSERVING
I, II Kings	• Historical background to understand written prophets. • God's constant intervention in events of history.
17 Prophetical Books	• Overall message of each book. • God's use of the prophets to change the course of history. • Truth which can be reapplied to our times. (Recommend beginning with Amos, Daniel as these are more easily studied hermeneutically. The minor prophets probably should be analyzed in depth, the major prophets surveyed.)
Gospels	• Jesus' prophetic voice to His people—never a compromise where truth was an issue. • Events, problems on which Jesus made strong stands. • Truth to be applied.
Romans 9-11	• God's way of correcting situations and using even the corrections in His plan. • God's warning to the church to produce or be set aside. • Truth to be applied.
I, II Thess.	• Essential truths about 2nd coming. • Trends that will occur in last days. • Warnings. • Paul's coupling of truth about 2nd coming with demands upon behavior. • Truth to be applied.
I Tim. 4:1-10 II Tim. 3:10-17	• Description of latter days. • Description of latter days. • Truth to be applied.
II Peter	• Stern warnings. • Descriptions of false teachers. • Truth to be applied.
Jude	• Stern warnings. • Descriptions of those exercising bad influences on Christianity. • Truth to be applied.
Revelation	• Tenor of God's intents. • Warnings.

comment | These are certainly not all the passages of value to one having the gift of prophecy, but they will do much to mold one's thinking as to God's use of the prophetical role as well as provide examples of warning and kinds of truth given through the prophetical voice.

HOW TO DEVELOP THE GIFT OF TEACHING

introduction   The gift of teaching ranks high among the leadership gifts. It
occurs by name in the three longer passages on gifts. God uses
this gift primarily to bring about maturity growth in the body.
Because a teacher has such an influence over many others there
must be constant searching of the Scriptures to insure that what
is being taught is truth. A teacher should be quick to modify
views whenever they are inconsistent with the teacher's ever-
increasing grasp of Scripture. James 3:1 warns that teachers
will receive greater judgement; people should carefully exercise
this gift. II Peter (and probably Jude) strongly warns against
the influence of false teachers. Any teacher can be a false
teacher in some given area of teaching. We must be careful to
heed this warning. Even though there are dangers that accompany
teaching there are great rewards. It is a tremendous thing to
realize that God has shown you truth and you can pass it on so
that others have their lives changed by it. The satisfaction of
seeing God's truth change lives is certainly reward enough for
one exercising this gift.

comment   In all that follows by way of suggestions it is assumed that
you are trusting the Holy Spirit to guide you into truth.
Principles, suggestions, and practices are lifeless apart from
the ministry of the Holy Spirit. On the other hand, the Spirit
does not work in a vacuum but utilizes basic principles to
guide us into truth.

G I V E N	You have the gift of teaching and want to develop it.	
STEP	PROCEDURE	PROCEDURAL FOLLOW-UP SUGGESTIONS
1.	MAKE CERTAIN YOU HAVE A FOUNDATIONAL UNDER-STANDING OF INTERPRE-TIVE PRINCIPLES TO GUIDE YOU IN YOUR STUDY OF THE BIBLE.	1. Master a system of hermeneutical principles based on the grammatical-historical approach to the Bible. 2. Study Bernard's Progress of Doctrine in order to learn the importance of interpreting a book in light of the progress of revelation. Transfer this kind of thinking to all the Bible. 3. It is recognized that teachers will operate at varying levels of ministry. Therefore, the extent to which they are exposed to the above concepts will vary. Every teacher, however, should at least be exposed at a popular level to the above concepts.

HOW TO DEVELOP THE GIFT OF TEACHING (cont.)

STEP	PROCEDURE	PROCEDURAL FOLLOW-UP SUGGESTIONS
2.	SYSTEMATICALLY BEGIN A PROGRAM TO MASTER THE BIBLE KEEPING IN MIND THAT YOU SHOULD BE A CONTINUAL SEARCHER FOR TRUTH.	1. Determine to master as much of the Bible as you can in your lifetime. If you lack discipline to study, ask God to give you a hunger to learn and the ability to study. By master is meant you can give the overall theme and purpose of a book and see your way completely through the book in order to relate structure to the theme. 2. Have a Bible reading program which you repeatedly use to familiarize yourself with the entire Bible. 3. Set up a plan to study in depth individual books of the Bible applying your hermeneutical system to each book. Always be mastering some book of the Bible. 4. Use a book like G. Campbell Morgan's Living Messages of the Books of the Bible in order to see significant contributions of each book in terms of truth which can be applied to each generation. 5. Make it a practice to try to do your own original study of a book before going to commentaries or other aids. 6. Use commentaries which follow the set of hermeneutical principles that you do.
3.	MAKE IT A PRIORITY TO APPLY ANY TRUTH YOU LEARN IN YOUR OWN LIFE	1. Be conscious in your Bible study that God is first dealing with you then those to whom you will minister. 2. Seek to be very practical in applying the Scriptures to your own life. 3. Remember when you speak from experience your teaching usually carries authoritative weight. (Maturity Appeal Leadership style) 4. What you are will speak as much as what you say. (Imitation Modeling Leadership Style).
4.	SYSTEMATICALLY MASTER PRINCIPLES OF COMMUNICATION AND VARIOUS METHODS TO APPLY THEM.	1. Study the Parables of Jesus to see principles of communication. 2. Study Gregory's Laws of Teaching and come back to them time and again to evaluate your own teaching with them. 3. Use a Receptor-oriented model of communication.

HOW TO DEVELOP THE GIFT OF TEACHING (cont.)

4.	(continued)	4.	Study Richard's books, Creative Bible Study, Creative Bible Teaching and a Theology of Christian Education. These books are loaded with practical help as well as underlying fundamental principles of learning. These books are especially helpful in helping you to become a facilitator-teacher.
5.	BE LEARNER CENTERED IN YOUR APPROACH TO TEACHING.	1.	Master feedback techniques and use them in all your teaching. Never be satisfied to only think that learning is going on.
		2.	Be conscious always of the learners in the teaching process. When you sense they aren't learning, find out why. Remember as a teacher you are responsible for the learner learning.
6.	BE CONSTANTLY UPDATING AND IMPROVING YOUR PRESENTATION OF MATERIAL	1.	Use objectives and lesson preparation sheets. (At least do so intuitively.)
		2.	Be flexible enough to change any presentation of any kind.
		3.	Evaluate each activity or method of presentation in terms of your objectives. Can it be improved?
7.	BE SUCCESS CENTERED BY DEMONSTRATING A WILLINGNESS TO TRY ANY INNOVATIVE TECHNIQUES IN ORDER TO COMMUNICATE SUCCESS FULLY.	1.	Your goal is to communicate so don't be afraid to try any approach to get your ideas across. If you fail you can always try again.
		2.	Timid teachers usually carry little influence.
8.	IF AT ALL POSSIBLE SPEND AN EXTENDED PERIOD OF TIME INVOLVED WITH A SUCCESSFUL TEACHER AND LEARN WHAT YOU CAN FROM HIM.	1.	Analyze every teacher for his good and bad features. Avoid the bad ones in your own ministry. Use the good ones where they become a natural part of you.
		2.	Talk a lot with other teachers and discuss successes and failures and techniques, etc.
		3.	Be particularly on the lookout for anyone who communicates on the emotional and volitional level. Learn techniques for doing this.
9.	USE YOUR GIFT OFTEN BOTH IN THE GATHERED AND DISPERSED CHURCH.	1.	In the gathered church your exercise will be usually situational. You should be open to give a teaching which aids the worship as opportunity arises.
		2.	In the dispersed church use your gift on a regular basis to bring about maturity in individuals or groups.

HOW TO DEVELOP THE GIFT OF WISDOM

introduction	In the Bible, wisdom usually increases with experience and maturity. And it is probably so in the case of the gift of wisdom. Time and again churches and individual church members will face situations which are complex and in which the direction to take is confusing. For just such situations God will have his man or woman who sees the way to go. The answers that God gives through this gift will usually be self-authenticating (that is, once given, there will be consensus agreement, or intuitive acceptance of it, etc.). It will also be the case that past experience with regard to advice through these gifted people will prove over and over that the answers were from God. The need for this gift is apparent. But few of the body are aware of or are willing to depend on God's choices for them through others.

G I V E N	You have the gift of wisdom and want to develop it to aid others.	
STEP	**PROCEDURE**	**PROCEDURAL FOLLOW-UP**
1.	DEVELOP AN OVERALL MASTERY OF BIBLICAL TRUTH.	1. See procedure 1 under Developing Gift of Discernment, p. 141. 2. See procedures 1,2 of Gift of Exhortation, p. 137.
2.	BE PARTICULARLY CAREFUL OF GUARDING YOUR DEVOTIONAL LIFE.	1. This gift requires a developed inner life with God and a quiet mystical sense of God's moment-by-moment presence in direction of one's actions and thoughts. 2. Learn to spend much time in prayer with God. James 1:5,6 should be a habit with you. 3. Specifically focus on books like Psalms and Proverbs in your devotional life. 4. The gift of wisdom becomes increasingly effective with maturity in your Christian life. Therefore, you should spend frequent times of evaluating your life with God to make sure no barriers are hindering your spiritual growth.

HOW TO DEVELOP THE GIFT OF WISDOM, (cont.)

STEP	PROCEDURE	PROCEDURAL FOLLOW-UP
3.	MAKE A SPECIAL STUDY OF THE BOOK OF PROVERBS AND JAMES.	1. Proverbs applies truth to life and sets the pattern for applied spiritual common sense. 2. In James note: emphasis of applying truth to everyday actions, dependence on God for the wisdom to do this, the description of wisdom and qualities in one who has it.
4.	IN SMALL GROUP DISCUSSIONS AND INDIVIDUAL CONVERSATIONS BE ALERT TO PROMPTINGS BY THE HOLY SPIRIT IN WHICH HE WILL CALL YOUR ATTENTION TO SITUATIONS OR PROBLEMS FOR WHICH HE WILL GIVE YOU CLEAR SOLUTIONS.	1. Take advantage of ejaculatory praying in the midst of talking to others "a la Nehemiah" (Neh. 2:4). Expect God to give on-the-spot answers. 2. Sometimes in the midst of a problem you will see as if by intuition the way to untangle the situation. Expect this to happen. 3. It is likely that the gift of wisdom, will be coupled with a leadership gift in order that decision-making in the church be influenced by this gift.

Related maps   see WORD OF WISDOM p. 60.

HOW TO DEVELOP THE GIFT OF KNOWLEDGE

introduction   The gift, <u>word of knowledge,</u> represents the capacity to receive supernaturally-revealed knowledge which otherwise could not or would not be known. The development of this gift probably comes in stages: stage 1, the awareness that God can reveal knowledge directly to one; stage 2, the recognition that God does that today; stage 3, the recognition that God is doing that to the person with the gift (that is, the increasing understanding that certain promptings, thoughts, etc. are revealed directly from the Spirit); stage 4, the conviction that God the Spirit wants you to reveal to others the Words of Knowledge that He gives; stage 5, an increased sensitivity to the varied promptings that the Holy Spirit may use to reveal a Word of Knowledge; stage 6, an increased degree of freedom to rest in and believe and use with conviction those Words of Knowledge God gives. Development of the gift is enhanced by being with like-gifted people in the context of their use of the gift.

G I V E N	You have the gift of knowledge and want to develop it.	
STEP	PROCEDURE	PROCEDURAL FOLLOW-UP
1.	STUDY THE POSSIBLE EXAMPLES OF THIS GIFT IN THE BIBLE.	1. Acts 5:3ff; 16:28; 18:9; 20:25,29,30; 21:10; 27:22-26. 2. Seek to identify many other possible words of knowledge in the New Testament. 3. For all of these possible examples study the context to derive principles of the use of word of knowledge.
2.	SEEK ON-THE-JOB TRAINING.	1. Identify those who have this gift. 2. Spend much time watching them use this gift. 3. Under their watchfulness use your gift. Ask them about your use of your gift. Get their advice and their instruction.
3.	MAKE A LIST OF WAYS THAT PEOPLE RECEIVE WORDS OF KNOWLEDGE.	1. I will list again the ways that I know of in which words of knowledge have been manifested: ● You see in your mind's eye newspaper-like headlines. ● You may hear an audible-like inner voice. ● You may see a picture-like scene in the mind. ● In healing situations, you may actually feel pain in an organ or part of the body which God wants to heal for someone.

related maps   see WORD OF KNOWLEDGE, p. 60.

HOW TO DEVELOP THE GIFT OF KNOWLEDGE (cont.)

STEP	PROCEDURE	PROCEDURAL FOLLOW-UP
3.	(cont.)	• Upon occasion, probably rarely, you may just start to speak and out comes a word of knowledge which you weren't aware of. 2. Be open to God's use of these various ways to give you a word of knowledge. Probably, it could be worded stronger: expect God to use the various ways to give you a word of knowledge.
4.	RECORD YOUR WORDS OF KNOWLEDGE AND USE THEM TO HELP YOU GROW.	1. Faith increases when we see that God does indeed use us for His purposes. By keeping a written record you can look back and have your faith increased. 2. Keep a record book of your words of knowledge which includes the word, place, context, date, and how God used it.

HOW TO DEVELOP THE GIFT OF EXHORTATION

introduction	Each of us in the body of Christ needs to be encouraged and yes, sometimes prodded along as we live out our Christian lives. At other times, we especially need to be comforted. God has given the gift of exhortation within the body to meet these needs. The gift of exhortation is a primary means whereby Christians are enabled by one another to live Christ-like lives amidst their everyday circumstances. This gift should be the gift of many in the body. In a number of the reciprocal commands we are told to exhort one another. The practical suggestions to develop this gift are based on using Scriptural patterns of exhortation as a guide for us in exercising this gift.

G I V E N	You have the gift of exhortation and want to develop it.

STEP	PROCEDURE	PROCEDURAL FOLLOW-UP
1.	STUDY REGULARLY THE PASSAGES OF SCRIPTURE WHICH ARE HEAVY IN APPLICATION.	1. Your regular Bible reading program should focus on these kind of passages. Your devotional life should focus on Scriptures which are applicational in nature. See Table of Passages Focusing on Application of Truth to Life, p. 139. 2. Seek to apply these Scriptures to your own life. Write down your personal applications and note your personal obedience to God. 3. Be particularly sensitive to the Holy Spirit. He will quite often emphasize Scriptures which will apply to current situations around you.
2.	STUDY BIBLE BOOKS WHICH WILL HELP YOU BECOME SENSITIVE TO PEOPLE'S NEEDS.	1. Read regularly in the Psalms and note: • The moods and changing experiences faced by people as they walk with God. • God's method of meeting men in these situations. • How you can use the various Psalms to bring comfort to those facing the same kind of situations. 2. Study Job to note: • How to and how not to empathize with those in suffering. • The stress on the sovereignty of God—this will be a foundational principle in comforting and encouraging people. 3. Study Ecclesiastes to see areas in which men seek satisfaction.

HOW TO DEVELOP THE GIFT OF EXHORTATION (cont.)

STEP	PROCEDURE	PROCEDURAL FOLLOW-UP
3.	USE EXTRA-BIBLICAL SOURCES WHICH WILL HELP YOU BECOME SENSITIVE TO PEOPLE'S NEEDS.	1. There are a number of popularized books dealing with applied psychological principles and inter-personal relationships. Use these to help you learn to be sensitive to others and their needs. 2. Be careful to compare suggestions from extra-Biblical sources with Scriptural principles where dealt with by the Bible.
4.	MEMORIZE VERSES WHICH WILL PROVE HELPFUL TO YOU AS YOU USE YOUR EXHORTIVE GIFT.	Examples Proverbs 9:8 10:17 11:14 15:28,31 17:10 20:5 25:11,12 26:4,5 27:5,6,9,17 John 14:26 16:13 II Cor. 1:3,4 12:9 Hebrews 10:24,25 James 1:22
5.	MAKE SURE YOU ARE CLEAR ON AN APPROACH TO APPLY SCRIPTURE	1. People will question you on how you know such and such is true and applies to the situation. 2. Set forth your approach to recognizing truth from Scripture and for using it in current situations. 3. Make sure you have an approach to disputed practices and Christian liberty since you will exercise your gift many times in regard to these areas.
6.	IN SMALL GROUP DISCUSSIONS AND IN-DIVIDUAL CONVER-SATIONS BE ALERT TO PROMPTINGS BY THE HOLY SPIRIT IN WHICH HE WILL CALL YOUR ATTENTION TO SITUATIONS OR PROBLEMS TO WHICH HE HAS PREVIOUSLY GIVEN YOU HELP. SHARE THESE.	1. The experiences you face will be particu-larly used of God to teach you lessons to be used with others. 2. You will find that you are unusually sen-sitive to lessons learned from others' experiences also. You will also notice quick recall of verses, past experiences, and principles from time to time in your discussions with others. 4. Share these with others always in love and with the principles of Phil. 3:15,16 in mind.
7.	TAKE ADVANTAGE OF OPPORTUNITIES IN SMALL GROUPS AND THE GATHERED CHURCH TO SHARE YOUR CURRENT EXPERIENCES WITH GOD.	1. Because of the nature of your gift you can expect an unusual sensitivity to God in everyday circumstances. 2. Your sharing of your everyday experiences will be used by God to meet others facing similar situations though you may not be aware of their situation. 3. Share in a God-centered way rather than an experience-centered way.

Related maps   see EXHORTATION, p.63

TABLE OF PASSAGES FOCUSING ON APPLICATION OF TRUTH TO LIFE

Books or Passages	As You Read or Study You should Focus on:
Proverbs	• practical advice for all kinds of daily living • verses telling how to give advice • truth for current situation
parables	• various central truths taught by each parable, most of these are fundamental principles of Christianity • Jesus' method in applying truth to situations • truth for current situation
other discourses in Gospels	• Jesus' method in applying truth to situations • truth for current situation
Romans 12-16	• principles of interrelationships between Christians • principles concerning disputed practices • principles concerning government • truth for current situation
I Cor.	• The entire book illustrates Paul's approach to various problems. Note principles for applying truth to problems. • truth which can be applied today
Gal. 1:6-10 2:1-21 3:1-5 5:13-6:10	• intensity needed when correcting serious problems • importance of taking a stand if essential truth is involved • fervor in admonishing and example of admonishing • truth for current situation
Eph. 4:1 6:23	• examples of exhortive teaching • truth from the content to apply to today's situation
Phil.	• how to share from your present experience so as to meet needs of others • exhortations to unity • truth for current situation
Col. 3,4	• examples of admonitions • truth for current situation
Heb. 2:1-4 3:7-4:13 5:11-6:20 10:26:39 12,13	• examples of admonition • the importance of prefacing admonition by teaching • truth to apply to current situation
James	• practical use of Scripture to life situations • use and misuse of tongue • description of practical wisdom and principles for applying it • truth for current situation

TABLE OF PASSAGES FOCUSING ON APPLICATION OF TRUTH TO LIFE (cont.)

Books or Passages	As You Read or Study You Should Focus On:
I Peter	• how God expects us to submit to him in various areas of our lives and hence have our faith strengthened • various areas of life that need to be brought into subjection • truth to apply to current situation
I,II,III John	• attitudes toward sin and truth • practical expressions of love • truth to be applied to current situation
Jude	• examples of strong warnings • truth to be applied to current situation

comment

While the above are not all the exhortive or applicational type of passages in the Scriptures, they are certainly representative of the kinds of passage that one with an exhortive gift ought to be reading, studying and using regularly.

Though the passages were listed to point out the location of exhortive or application Scripture, bear in mind these passages as all passages in Scripture should be read in light of the context of the book as a whole of which they are a part.

HOW TO DEVELOP THE GIFT OF DISCERNMENT

introduction	The gift of discernment is God's method of guarding truth for his people. God will use this gift in the local church to insure that interpretation and use of Scripture is correct. In the regional church God will use this gift in order to formulate major doctrinal stands as he has done down through church history. Satanic activity is particularly directed toward perversion of truth. God specifically combats this with the gift of discernment. How important this gift is! Combined with one or more of the regional leadership gifts, the gift of discernment can influence large numbers of God's people toward truth. This gift along with the gift of miracles is mightily used of God in power encounters with the supernatural. Major breakthroughs in the spread of Christianity can come through confrontation with demonic forces—one focus of the gift, discerning of spirits. In the procedures that follow I will give suggestions for the indirect use of this gift—that of discerning of truth—and the direct use of this gift—that of discerning the source of the truth, the spirit world.

G I V E N	You have the gift, discerning of spirits, and want to develop it over your life-time.	
STEP	PROCEDURE	PROCEDURAL FOLLOW-UP
1.	DEVELOP AN OVERALL MASTERY OF BIBLICAL TRUTH.	1. See teaching procedures 1,2 pages 130, 131. 2. You must read through the Bible regularly and often as all the content of the Bible should be fresh to you and available to recall. 3. Know whether something is or is not mentioned or dealt with in Scripture. Learn to neither add to nor take away from that which is actually present in Scripture. Be satisfied to be just as clear as the Bible is clear.
2.	DEVELOP AND USE PRACTICAL TECHNIQUES OF HERMENEUTICS.	1. As your grasp of Biblical truth deepens you will find yourself doing more and more detailed study of smaller passages. 2. You must develop practical techniques which become second nature for you to use since you must increasingly become faster in Bible study because you are becoming more detailed.

HOW TO DEVELOP THE GIFT OF DISCERNMENT (cont.)

STEP	PROCEDURE	PROCEDURAL FOLLOW-UP
3.	DEVELOP THE RIGHT KIND OF QUESTIONING SPIRIT	1. Seek an attitude which wants to know truth. Avoid a critical spirit toward people—concentrate on the issue of truth. 2. Seek always to apply truth in a loving manner for the good of all. 3. Develop listening skills and the ability to question tactfully.
4.	DEVELOP SKILLS OF ANALYSIS	1. Study materials and books dealing with principles of logic and reasoning. 2. Learn skills which aid logical thinking (such as techniques of flow charting).
5.	STUDY IN-DEPTH MATERIALS DEALING WITH SPIRITS.	1. Study I John 4:1-5 to understand the spiritual principles of discerning of spirits. 2. Study the Gospels for Jesus' handling of spirits. List principles you see in his ministry. 3. Study modern writers who have analyzed the whole doctrine of the demonic world. See Kurt Koch's works for example.
6.	BE CAREFUL IN DEALING WITH THE SPIRIT WORLD.	1. Be cautioned that dealing with the spirit world opens you up to especially strong attacks. Be sure that if you enter in to ministry involving discerning of spirits you will need to have some powerful prayer backing to cover you in this ministry. 2. If you do not also have the gift of miracles then seek to team up with one who does have this gift as power encounters are likely to occur. 3. Be ready to rely on God's unusual power available in prayer. Be a person of prayer yourself. 4. Perhaps before dealing directly with the spirit world you should get some on-the-job training with people who have used discerning of spirits directly with the spirit world.

HOW TO DEVELOP THE GIFT OF DISCERNMENT (cont.)

7.	SEEK OPPORTUNITY TO EXERCISE YOUR GIFT	1. In the local church concentrate on correcting poor interpretation and application of Scripture. 2. If you have also a prophetical gift (sometimes the gift of discernment will be coupled with the prophetical gift) be alert to God's using you in the regional church to have a wider influence of correcting heretical tendencies in doctrine and practice. 3. It may be that you should develop writing skills in order that your gift will have larger influence in the regional church. 4. In dealing directly with the spirit world you will not normally have to seek opportunity. It will be brought to you.

comment   The gift of discernment probably more than any other gift demands a person who is willing to discipline himself to Bible study. It will take a lifetime to develop this gift. One with this kind of gift should seriously think of preserving what God has taught him over a life-time in literature available to God's people.

warning   This gift carries with it serious responsibility. On the one hand you must exercise extreme caution for you are sitting in on judgement of truth. And yet on the other hand, you can not afford to neglect this needed ministry to the church.

warning   Frequently those who deal directly with the spirit world become entrapped and eventually may come under bondage to spirits. If you enter in to this aspect of the gift of discerning of spirits, guard your inner life, guard your prayer life, and make sure you can use the power of God to confront.

related map   see DISCERNMENT, page 67.

HOW TO DEVELOP THE GIFT OF FAITH

introduction The gift of faith is one of the most exciting gifts to possess
and exercise since it depends upon the direct intervention of
God in human affairs. It is primarily exercised in solitude
alone with God. It may never receive the public acclaim that
other outward expressed gifts do, but there is more than reward
enough in the personal satisfaction enjoyed in the use of this
gift. For each time this special gift is exercised there is
that fresh definite confirmation again of the working power and
the real existence of God. And there is the certainty deep
within the soul of the reality of God and of one's own personal
relationship with him.

G I V E N	You have the gift of faith. Therefore, you must develop it.	
STEP	PROCEDURE	PROCEDURAL FOLLOW-UP SUGGESTIONS
1.	INCREASE YOUR KNOWLEDGE OF A MIGHTY AND WONDER-WORKING GOD AS REVEALED IN THE SCRIPTURES.	1. Study Biblically the concept of faith. 2. Have a regular Bible reading program which covers those portions of Scripture which stress God's historical working. Cover yearly: Gen. 12-25:10, 37-50; Ex. 1-24; Deut. 1-4,7-12,20,28-32; Joshua; Judges; I,II Sam; I,II Ki.; Matthew-Acts. As you read note particularly the special instances in which God intervened in a special way in the lives of his people. Note the kind of situations, barriers overcome, and final results. Answer specifically two questions about these portions. What have I learned about God? Faith? 3. Do in-depth book analyses of the following books: Joshua, Habakkuk, Daniel, John. 4. Do in-depth studies of the following Scripture portions: Num. 13,14; Deut. 1; II Ki. 6:8-7:20; I Chron. 4:9,10; Luke 11:1-13, 18:1-8; Romans 4; Hebrews 11. 5. Do a topical study on prayer listing principles, conditions, and promises which relate. 6. Spend much of your devotional time in the Psalms.

HOW TO DEVELOP THE GIFT OF FAITH (cont.)

STEP	PROCEDURE	PROCEDURAL FOLLOW-UP SUGGESTIONS
2.	INCREASE YOUR KNOWLEDGE OF GOD BY EXTRA-BIBLICAL STUDIES.	1. Study in depth the attributes of God commonly called the incommunicable attributes (most particularly the omni-attributes). Use a theological text to help you. 2. Study biographically the following characters (either Bible or writings of men like F.B. Meyer): Abraham, Joseph, Moses, Elijah, Elisha, Samuel. 3. Read books such as the following of great Christians who evidenced the gift of faith: George Mueller of Bristol by A.T. Pierson, Behind the Ranges (story of J.O. Fraser) by Mrs. Howard Taylor, the two volumes on Hudson Taylor's life, The Growth of a Soul, The Growth of a Work of God, both by Mrs. Howard Taylor; Rees Howell-Intercessor by Norman Grubb. 4. Read books on knowing God such as Knowing God by J.I. Packer, The Knowledge of the Holy by A.W. Tozer. 5. Read books on prayer.
3.	MAINTAIN A RECORD OF YOUR PRAYER LIFE IN ORDER TO ENCOURAGE YOUR TRUST IN GOD.	1. Use a prayer notebook with a prayer schedule. Review and update schedule regularly. 2. Keep a record of specific requests which represent special ventures of faith. Note answers to these specific ventures of faith. Date requests and answers.
4.	BECOME CONSCIOUS OF AND USE THE PROMISES OF THE WORD OF GOD	1. In your prayer notebook keep a list of promises. 2. In your reading and study of the Bible seek to note promises which are general in nature or conditional but which conditions you can meet. 3. Review this list of promises regularly in terms of situations around you. 4. Ask God to make these promises real for you. Record special instances in which God speaks to you in these promises.
5.	PRAY TOGETHER WITH A SPECIAL PRAYER PARTNER WHO ALSO HAS THE GIFT OF FAITH.	1. Ask God to bring this kind of partner to you. 2. Meet regularly with this prayer partner. 3. Covenant together in each special venture in faith to wait upon God and to support each other until God works.

HOW TO DEVELOP THE GIFT OF FAITH (cont.)

STEP	PROCEDURE	PROCEDURAL FOLLOW-UP SUGGESTIONS
6.	MEMORIZE SCRIPTURES WHICH WILL ENCOURAGE THE GIFT OF FAITH.	1. Examples of these kinds of Passages: Matt. 7:7-11 21:21,22 18:19 Mark 9:23, 24 11:22-24 John 14:12-14 15:7 16:23, 24 Rom. 4:20,21 Hebrews 11.
7.	BE ESPECIALLY ALERT TO RELATE SITUATIONS AROUND YOU WITH PROMISES AND PRAYER REQUESTS WHICH WILL EXTEND YOU TO DEPEND UPON GOD.	Ways in which you can be alert: 1. In your ministry seek and expect to find situations which will need one who can confidently believe God for solutions. 2. For each such situation ask God for a promise from His word or confirmations from His word on what He wants to do. 3. Claim his working even though others around you may not be able to step out in faith in the same way. 4. Once you are convinced of God's working do all you can to encourage those around you that God will work. 5. Spearhead a prayer effort for this working of God. 6. If need be stand alone in prayer and trust in God until you see God accomplishing what you believed him for.

comment   This gift is always greatly needed within the church. It is particularly used by God to exhort the church to pray and believe in a prayer-answering God. It is also used by God to encourage the church in special times of need. And then too, it is through the exercise of this gift that God intervenes directly in the lives of his people when he wants to do some special work.

building
up
faith   Dependence upon God is the very essence of this gift. The nature of this gift is such that its exercise in power increases with the maturity of the believer and the growth of personal experience and knowledge of God. Therefore, the suggestions for development of this gift hinge around those things which will increase one's knowledge of, experience with and confidence in, a mighty and sovereign God. Biblical studies, extra-Biblical studies and practical helps all focus on building one's dependence upon God so that the gift of faith will be exercised more and more.

related map   see FAITH, page 69.

HOW TO DEVELOP THE GIFT OF GIVING

introduction   God has a way to meet the needs of his people. Normally it is through the gifts of his people who demonstrate their care and concern for one another. Giving is a natural outflow of Christian love. However, God has placed within the body men and women who have the special gift of giving. These God will use **not** only as a part of his normal means of meeting needs but will also use these gifts to meet needs that will **not** be met any other way. This gift offers rewards of joy in seeing needs met that will **not** be experienced by many. But this gift has its dangers. One who is used by God to channel finances into Christian work must be aware that Satan will always be tempting to sidetrack one into appropriating rather than dispensing that which God provides.

G I V E N	You sense that God wants to use you in a special way to channel finances to others.	
STEP	PROCEDURE	PROCEDURAL FOLLOW-UP
1.	MAKE IN DEPTH STUDIES OF CERTAIN SPECIFIC PASSAGES WHICH SHOULD MOLD YOUR THINKING TOWARD GOD'S USE OF THIS GIFT IN YOU.	1. Study the parables of the Unjust Steward and the Rich Man and Lazarus. 2. Read the passages in Acts which are given to illustrate the gift of giving. 3. Study 2 Cor 8,9 which gives the exhaustive treatment of New Testament teaching on giving. 4. Study Philippians in general which is a thank-you note to some who gave. Specifically concentrate on Phil. 4:10-19. 5. Study in depth I Tim. 6:3-10. 6. Study James 5:1-6. 7. Memorize the following: Rom. 12:8 Gal 6:6 Eph. 4:28b Phil. 4:19 II Cor. 9:7,8 Jas. 2:2-4 I John 3:17. In all of the above passages ask God to give you principles and convictions which you will hold on to through life.

HOW TO DEVELOP THE GIFT OF GIVING (cont.)

STEP	PROCEDURE	PROCEDURAL FOLLOW-UP
2.	RECOGNIZE THAT GOD MAY HAVE GIVEN YOU SPECIAL ABILITIES TO USE FOR HIM.	1. Dedicate your business abilities to God. In one sense it is your full-time Christian service, for you are his special steward. 2. As a part of your ministry for God, you should develop your abilities—schooling, whatever. This should be a priority for you. 3. Seek special guidance concerning the business or business partners you will associate with. Ask God for a like-minded partner. 4. You can expect unusual miracles in your business.
3.	RECOGNIZE THAT IF GOD HAS NOT GIVEN YOU SPECIAL ABILITIES HE CAN STILL UTILIZE THE GIFT OF GIVING THROUGH YOU.	1. If you don't particularly have great resources or abilities to earn money, God can still use you if you desire to give to help others. You will find that God may have given you ability to live comfortably with less than most so that by carefulness you are able to give more. 2. God often couples the gift of giving with the gift of faith to bring finances to you so that you can direct them to others. 3. Claim II Cor. 8:12 (expecting God to use the gift regardless of its size) and II Cor. 9:6-15 (expecting God to provide to meet the needs).
4.	RECOGNIZE THAT YOU WILL HAVE UNUSUAL SENSITIVITY TO NEEDS.	1. Because of the nature of your gift you will find that God will bring to your attention needs that average Christians do not sense. 2. Ask God to teach you to welcome these as opportunities for him to work through you.
5.	DON'T LIMIT GOD BY CEASING TO GIVE FREELY.	1. Keep the channel open. Never keep for your own personal use that which God has indicated is for someone else. 2. As your gift of giving increases you can expect to be drawn into exercise of it in the regional church.

related map   see GIVING, page 71.

HOW TO DEVELOP THE GIFT OF APOSTLESHIP

introduction	E.M. Bounds said, "We are constantly on a stretch, if not on a strain, to devise new methods, new plans, new organizations to advance the church and secure enlargement and efficiency for the Gospel. This trend of the day has a tendency to lose sight of the man or sink the man in the plan or organization. God's plan is to make much of the man, far more of him than of anything else. Men are God's method. The church is looking for better methods; God is looking for better men." This is the essence of the gift of apostleship—a man sent from God; a man who will reach peoples for Christ and begin new churches, whether in the ghetto, the city, suburbs or rural areas, home or abroad; a man who is willing to sacrifice, if necessary, to get the job done. We echo with E.M. Bounds--men are God's method. The essence of the apostolic function is a man called of God who has the capacity to begin works of God. He will usually be multi-gifted. The suggestions below are general and help develop background needed for a man through whom God can exercise the gift of apostleship.

G I V E N	You have the gift of apostleship and want to be developing yourself for greater use.	
STEP	PROCEDURE	PROCEDURAL FOLLOW-UP SUGGESTIONS
1.	DEVELOP A CLEAR UNDERSTANDING OF THE NATURE OF THE CHURCH, ITS PURPOSES, FUNCTIONS, AND GROWTH PROCESSES.	1. Do a formal or informal course of study to determine your Biblical view of the church. 2. Associate yourself with someone now being used of God in the Church Renewal movement and study and discuss with him concerning Biblical views of the church. 3. Spend time with colleagues of like mind in exchanging ideas on the church.
2.	BE AN ALL-AROUND BIBLE STUDENT BUT MASTER BY IN-DEPTH STUDIES SPECIAL PASSAGES.	1. You should master the pastoral epistles. 2. You should master the church epistles. 3. You should master the selected leadership passages from other portions of Scripture. 4. You should master the book of Acts.

HOW TO DEVELOP THE GIFT OF APOSTLESHIP (cont.)

STEP	PROCEDURE	PROCEDURAL FOLLOW-UP SUGGESTIONS
3.	MAKE A SPECIAL STUDY OF THE SPIRITUAL QUAL-IFICATIONS OF AN ELDER AND APPLY THESE STAND-ARDS TO YOUR OWN LIFE.	1. You must model these standards. 2. You will use these standards to se-lect leadership for the church you are founding.
4.	DEVELOP A MIND-SET FOR STRATEGIZING.	1. Learn skills of goal setting, priori-tizing, planning and evaluating. Then develop a very flexible attitude which can recognize the Spirit's confirmation or setting aside of plans. 2. Study the revival movements in church history to draw out principles which can be reapplied. 3. Study the major movements in missions in the last 30 years: church growth, saturation evangelism, theological educa-tion by extension, church renewal, lay involvements, etc.
5.	READ WIDELY.	1. Learn to read selectively. 2. Read books on applied ecclesiology. 3. Read books on church growth. 4. Read books on personal renewal. 5. Read missionary biographies. Look for: a challenge from God, examples of God giving men vision, principles of building a work of God. 6. Read books in applied anthropology and sociology. More and more Christian au-thors and groups are writing in this field.
6.	GET ON-THE-JOB TRAINING WITH EXPERTS.	1. Find a church which is demonstrating the philosophy of the church which you have come to understand. Ask God to open a way for you to move in to the situation and be used in it. 2. Find a successful church planter who you feel is exercising the apostolic function and ask him to take you into his ministry for a period of training.
7.	WORK PRIMARILY IN THE REGIONAL CHURCH.	1. Make certain you are under authority from a local church. 2. Keep flexible so that God can move you to new places.

Related Map   see APOSTLESHIP, page 75

HOW TO DEVELOP THE GIFT OF EVANGELISM

introduction	One of the most exciting happenings in the world is the introduction of new people to the living Christ and having them respond to Him and become a part of his Church. There is a tremendous joy associated with seeing people transformed by a living Christ. Paul said of the Thessalonican Christians, "For what is our hope, or joy, or crown of rejoicing? Are not even ye in the presence of our Lord Jesus Christ at his coming?" Some will have this gift and can use it publicly with mighty results. Some will quietly in harmony with others and/or in individual situations see people come to Christ.
spectrum	The gift of evangelism can be viewed as different aspects which taken together support the total task of "persuading" men to become Christians. Some possessing the gift will be strong in one or more aspects, others in other aspects. A few will be strong in all aspects. However, people working together and utilizing their strengths will in concert see results. Here is an overview of the spectrum of evangelism.

prayer evangelism	friendship evangelism	confrontation evangelism	teaching evangelism	public evangelism	follow-through evangelism

——— low key ———→   ——— high key ———→ — clinching —→

G I V E N	You have the gift of evangelism and want to develop it.	
STEP	**PROCEDURE**	**PROCEDURAL FOLLOW-UP**
1.	MAKE CERTAIN YOU ARE CLEAR ON THE ESSENTIALS OF SALVATION.	1. Do Biblical studies to clarify your understanding of salvation. 2. Study the various passages in Acts in which people are confronted with the Gospel, taking into account the progress of doctrine. Jot down what it was that recipients of Christ were asked to do and what they did to respond to Christ.

HOW TO DEVELOP THE GIFT OF EVANGELISM (cont.)

STEP	PROCEDURE	PROCEDURAL FOLLOW-UP
2.	USE THE SPECTRUM ABOVE AND BEGIN WITH LOW KEY EVANGELISM MOVING TOWARD HIGH KEY EVANGELISM.	1. Join a group or team in your church which is interested in evangelism. 2. Find the aspect of evangelism that allows you as part of the team to contribute effectively. 3. Make certain that no matter whatever aspect of evangelism you personally emphasize that people being evangelized can be taken through the whole spectrum.
3.	TAKE ADVANTAGE OF VARIOUS TRAINING PROGRAMS.	1. Bible colleges, institutes offer courses in evangelism. 2. Various organizations specialize in evangelism and offer different training programs. 3. Various training programs will teach skills and methods of confronting people with Christ. 4. Many books are written on the subject.
4.	MAKE CERTAIN THAT YOU GET ON-THE-JOB EXPERIENCE WITH AN EVANGELISTIC TEAM OR PERSON HAVING EVANGELISTIC GIFTS.	1. If your church has a ministry team which focuses on evangelism, join it. 2. Spend time with a man or woman who evidences this gift and learn practically to share Christ with others.
5.	BECOME PEOPLE-CENTERED IN YOUR THINKING.	1. Spend a good bit of devotional time in the Gospel of Luke (and other Gospels). 2. Read books which develop in you a concern for people.

Related maps   see EVANGELISM, page 78

HOW TO DEVELOP THE PASTORAL GIFT

introduction	When one reads the Kings and Chronicles it is apparent that leadership determines the way a nation will go. If the leader is a man of God the nation will progress spiritually; if he is spiritually weak the nation suffers. So it is with any group. God recognizes the need for leadership and has provided for it in his church. The pastoral gift particularly focuses on leadership at local church level. Strong leadership is needed if the church is to exist successfully in our day.

G I V E N	You want to develop and use your pastoral gift to produce results for God.	
STEP	PROCEDURE	PROCEDURAL FOLLOW-UP
1.	MAKE A SPECIAL STUDY OF LEADERSHIP PASSAGES IN SCRIPTURE IN ORDER TO KNOW AND USE GOD'S LEADERSHIP STANDARDS IN YOUR MINISTRY.	1. See Table of Leadership Passages, p. 155 2. Ask God to put the results of your study into your life. 3. Memorize some key leadership verses: Proverbs 11:14; 22:3 Acts 20:28; I Thess. 5:12,13; Gal. 6:1,2; Heb. 13:7,17.
2.	DEVELOP A CLEAR UNDER-STANDING OF THE NATURE OF THE CHURCH, ITS PURPOSES, FUNCTIONS, AND GROWTH PROCESSES.	Study in detail the doctrine of the church with fellow elders and especially one who has the gift of teaching. You should be aware that God is doing a special work in the Church as a whole in terms of applied ecclesiology in our day.
3.	MAKE A SPECIAL STUDY OF THE SPIRITUAL QUALIFICATIONS OF AN ELDER AND APPLY THESE STANDARDS TO YOUR OWN LIFE.	1. You must model these standards. 2. You must exert influence by your life-style.
4.	BE AN ALL-AROUND BIBLE STUDENT BUT MASTER BY IN-DEPTH STUDIES SPECIAL PASSAGES.	1. See particularly steps 1,2 under gift of discernment, p. 141. 2. You should master the pastoral epistles. 3. You should master the church epistles. 4. You should master the selected leadership passages from other Bible portions. 5. You should master the book of Acts.

HOW TO DEVELOP THE PASTORAL GIFTS (cont.)

STEP	PROCEDURE	PROCEDURAL FOLLOW-UP
5.	STUDY BIBLE BOOKS AND OTHER BOOKS WHICH WILL HELP YOU BECOME SENSITIVE TO PEOPLE'S NEEDS.	1. The concept of shepherding involves caring for and meeting the needs of people. 2. Use the detailed procedures under steps 1, 2, 3, of developing exhortive gift (p. 137).
6.	STUDY BIOGRAPHICALLY GREAT CHRISTIAN LEADERS LOOKING FOR UNDERLYING LEADERSHIP PRINCIPLES.	1. Study the following Bible characters: Abraham, Joseph, Moses, Elijah, Elisha, Samuel, Paul. F. B. Meyer has a series of helpful books on these characters. 2. Read Christian biographies looking for leadership principles.

Related maps   see THE PASTORAL GIFT, p. 57
                see also TABLE OF LEADERSHIP PASSAGES, p. 155

TABLE OF LEADERSHIP PASSAGES

Books, Passages, Individuals	As You Read or Study You Should Focus on:	Method of Approach
Matt. 18:15-20	• Principles of Discipline	Shared in-depth study with elders
Acts 20:17-38	• Principles of leadership that Paul modelled • Responsibilities of leadership	Shared in-depth study with elders
I Cor.	• Responsibility for founding and developing a work of God • Principles dealing with church problems • Importance of discipline	Shared in-depth study with elders
II Cor.	• Principles of dependence on the grace of God in leadership • Discouragement in leadership	Read as part of devotional life
Gal. 6:1-10	• Responsibility toward those in spiritual trouble	In-depth study with elders
Phil.	• Principles of a leader motivating others • Principles dealing with unity	Read as part of devotional life
Pastoral Epistles	• Foundational principles of leadership • Standards for elders	An in-depth study with elders and with one having gift of teaching
Philemon	• How to deal with a problem tactfully • Paul as a Christian gentleman • The leadership style called Obligation-persuasion	Read as part of devotional life
I Pet. 5:1-11	• Warnings against over-authoritative leadership • Place of humility and submissiveness in leadership	In-depth study with elders
Joseph Moses Joshua David	• Principles showing how God makes a man of God	Read popular biographies such as F. B. Meyer's condensed versions or do your own biographical study

LIST OF PRACTICAL WAYS TO EXERCISE YOUR GIFT

Gift	Activity in Traditional Church (role)	Activity in Interdependent Gift-oriented Church (role)	Activity in Regional Church (role)
prophecy	• pulpit ministry (pastor) • Wednesday Prayer Meeting (staff) • radio ministry (full-time staff worker)	• special called services (anyone) • Sunday Worship (anyone) • radio ministry (member of communications team) • ministry groups (anyone)	• para-church structures (full-time worker) • radio ministry (usually recognizable full-time worker) • writing ministry (anyone who can get backing) • conference/retreat speaker (usually one of renown)
teaching	• Sunday School (anyone) • pulpit (pastor or assistant pastor) • radio (staff worker)	• all kinds of ministry groups (anyone) • training groups (anyone) • retreat ministry (anyone) • Bible conference (anyone) • radio ministry (member of communications team)	• Bible Conferences (full-time worker of renown) • para-church educational institutes (full-time worker with special educational qualifications)
knowledge wisdom	• occasionally with individuals (anyone) • pastoral counselling (full-time worker) • various committees (anyone)	• ministry groups of all kinds (anyone) • frequently with individuals (anyone) • leadership groups (anyone) • counselling teams (anyone)	• boards of para-church structures (people of renown)
exhortation	• occasionally with individuals (anyone) • pastoral counselling (full-time worker) • Sunday School classes	• counselling teams (anyone) • ministry groups of all kinds (anyone) • frequently with individuals (anyone) • retreats (anyone)	• retreats in conjunction with para-church structures (primarily people of renown)

LIST OF PRACTICAL WAYS TO EXERCISE YOUR GIFT (cont.)

Gift	Activity in Traditional Church (role)	Activity in Interdependent Church (role)	Activity in Regional Church (role)
discernment	• selection of training materials (Christian Education Director or equivalent)	• in all teaching functions with all kinds of small groups (anyone) • evaluation team (anyone) • communications team (anyone) • worship team (anyone)	• writing (anyone who can get backing) • para-church groups producing literature (people who can meet qualifications to be hired)
faith	• individually (anyone)	• individually (anyone) • ministry groups (anyone) • faith teams (anyone)	• para-church structures (entrepreneurs)
giving	• regular church programs (anyone) • extra-church social programs (anyone) • sometimes to individual missionaries (anyone)	• regular church programs (anyone) • through mercy teams (anyone) • to other individuals in church (anyone) • through mission teams (anyone) • to individual missionaries (anyone)	• to para-church structures (anyone) • to missionaries (anyone) • to social programs (anyone)
apostleship	• through denominational or interdenominational sending groups	• church planting team (anyone) • individual under authority of church	• through para-church groups
pastoring	• receive call as pastor	• as shepherd or undershepherd responsible for group and in mutual submission to other shepherds	• through para-church groups

LIST OF PRACTICAL WAYS TO EXERCISE YOUR GIFT (cont.)

Gift	Activity in Traditional Church (role)	Activity in Interdependent Gift-oriented Church (role)	Activity in Regional Church (role)
evangel- ism	• pulpit min- istry (pastor) • some lay witness programs (anyone) • individuals (anyone) • radio ministry (staff)	• church planting teams (anyone) • outreach teams (anyone) • communications teams (anyone) • mercy teams (anyone) • evangelism small groups (anyone) • body evangelism (all) • radio ministry (anyone) • individuals (anyone)	• public cam- paigns (full- time recognized evangelist) • para-church structures (missionary) • radio ministry (usually recog- nized full-time worker)
mercy	• food baskets at various holiday seasons (any- one) • some finances go to this sometimes (anyone) • coffee houses for reaching teens with drug problems (anyone)	• mercy teams in- volved in literacy, hos- pital, drug problems, edu- cational pro- grams, prison work, alcoholics, etc. (anyone)	• para-church structures em- phasizing social outreach (anyone)
govern- ments	• ruling struc- tures (usually full-time workers and older influen- tial business- men) • various minor committees (anyone)	• ruling struc- ture (represent- atives of teams and groups)	• mission structures (leadership)
helps	• volunteers for various pro- grams (anyone)	• ministry groups • worship team • music team • almost any team	• para-church struc- tures (short term specialized)

SOME FINAL SUGGESTIONS

what we
were
intending
to do

How well have you done in learning what you should have learned form this study on spiritual gifts?
Two suggestions:

- Read back over section and module preview pages.
- Read the block on objectives. Have you met these?

But more important than mastering the contents of this booklet, you should know your gift(s) and have made plans to develop them.

In Section I we suggested a fourfold procedure for profiting on teaching on Spiritual Gifts.

1. Identify your gift (Section II).
2. Set out a plan to develop your gift (Section III).
3. Choose your service in terms of your gift.
4. Use your gift.

We have set forth some help for procedures 1,2. Now for a word on 3. The church is central in God's plan. How you relate to it should be determined by your gift(s). Under God you must develop and exercise the gifts He has given. You must choose a church structure or mission structure which allows you freedom to do so. Your choice of vocation should be made in light of your service to the church. For some, their gifts may demand some full-time Christian vocation in order that their gifts be fully utilized. For others, their gifts can best be fully used of God without a full-time Christian vocation.

Now to procedure 4.

4. Use your gift.

This one is up to you. May you experience joy in being part of a church which is "people functioning interdependently according to their unique Christ-given gifts, and ministering one to the other in love."

FEEDBACK ON SECTION III.

your
intentions

List here some "short range" intents you have for developing
your gift(s).

What long range implications have resulted for you as a result
of your study on Spiritual gifts?

GROUP STUDY-GUIDE

PREVIEW: SECTION IV. GROUP STUDY GUIDE

introduction   Section IV is a 13 lesson study guide intended for a Sunday
School class format. The lesson guides give the objectives of
each lesson and the various activities and assignments that
class members should do. The lesson will refer the student to
the relevant portions of Sections I, II, and III that need to be
read. The design for each class lesson assumes about 45 minutes
of class time. It also assumes that a student will spend 30 to
90 minutes outside of class in preparing for a lesson. The
class teacher can afford to be a facilitator if students do
prepare before hand. This means that class time can be spent on
dynamic reflection--that is, clarification, application, and
value forming exercises. The 13 lessons cover all three
sections of Spiritual Gifts. However, the identification
Section (II) and the development Section (III) do not receive as
much attention as I would like. If your class has more time
than 13 sessions then I would recommend that the lessons dealing
with identification and development be expanded.

contents   <u>Description</u>
Section IV

PREVIEW

UNIT 1: BACKGROUND ON SPIRITUAL GIFTS
    LESSON 1. WHO NEEDS SPIRITUAL GIFTS ANYWAY?
    LESSON 2. USE HOLY CAUTION IN YOUR STUDY
    SUMMARY OF UNIT 1

UNIT 2: BIBLICAL PASSAGES--LISTING OF GIFTS
    LESSON 3. CONFUSION AT CORINTH--I CORINTHIANS 12-14
    LESSON 4. REACHING OUT FROM ROME--ROMANS 12
    LESSON 5. THE BIG PICTURE--EPHESIANS 4
    LESSON 6. PUTTING IT TOGETHER--COMPARATIVE STUDY
    SUMMARY OF UNIT 2

UNIT 3: DEFINITIONS
    LESSON 7. MATURITY GROWTH GIFTS
    LESSON 8. NUMERICAL GROWTH GIFTS
    LESSON 9. ORGANIC GROWTH GIFTS
    SUMMARY OF UNIT 3

UNIT 4: RECOGNIZING GIFTS IN PEOPLE
    LESSON 10. MY VIEW OF MY GIFT(S)
    LESSON 11. OTHER'S VIEW OF MY GIFT(S)
    LESSON 12. MY VIEW OF THE GIFTS OF OTHERS
    SUMMARY OF UNIT 4

UNIT 5: USING WHAT I HAVE LEARNED
    LESSON 13. PLANS TO DEVELOP AND USE MY GIFT

SUMMARY OF ALL UNITS
ADVICE TO THE GROUP LEADER

LESSON 1. WHO NEEDS SPIRITUAL GIFTS ANYWAY?

introduction   Who needs spiritual gifts anyway? I do. You do. Our churches do. Perhaps you don't think so yet. But let me phrase the question another way. Who wants to attempt God's work without using God's provision? I hope no one. And yet we may well be doing that if we are not taking advantage of one of God's wonderful provisions for the church--spiritual gifts. This lesson introduces us to the notion of spiritual gifts, the ways they can help us in the church, some basic reasons why you yourself should study the important doctrine of spiritual gifts, and some implications about spiritual gifts.

purpose   The purpose of Lesson 1 is to motivate you to know and use your own spiritual gift with and for other believers. Lesson 1 should lead you to recognize that spiritual gifts are God's provision for the local church to bring about healthy growth. As a result of lesson 1 you should look forward to this course. It is both an opportunity and a challenge from God.

objectives   Here is what you can hope to have accomplished by the time you
lesson 1   finish this lesson:

- you will be able to define the concept of spiritual gift so that if given a list of 4 of the 5 concepts involved in the definition of a spiritual gift you will be able to give in your own words the missing concept.

- you will be able to match the multi-dimensions of church growth (to which spiritual gifts contribute) to statements describing these important kinds of growth,

- you will be able to list from the 4 reasons given for studying spiritual gifts the reason most applicable to you as well as tell why it is so.

- you will have selected 5 implications about spiritual gifts as ones for which you want further information in your future study of this topic. Hopefully by the end of the 13 lessons you'll have some answers on these.

choice of   Where time is limited you can expect your group study
assignments   leader to select from the list which follows. Where adequate time is available you should do all of the assignments. Check with your group study leader on just which assignments you should do.

pre-study   Before you begin the assignments listed below why don't you read
assignment   the article which follows the assignment list. It will introduce the notion of spiritual gifts and of interdependent ministry. Perhaps it will show you how much or how little you already know about gifts.

ASSIGNMENT CHECK-OFF LIST

instructions   Below are the possible assignments for lesson 1. Do the ones
assigned by your group leader.

Motivation Exercise To Be Done Before Other Assignments

____ Read the Article "Gifts Are For Sharing" by Bobby Clinton and
see how much you already know about gifts before you do the
rest of the assignments below.

Reading from Section I To Be Done Prior To Class

____ 4 REASONS FOR KNOWING YOUR GIFT, page 15.
____ SPIRITUAL GIFT, page 23.
____ 3 KINDS OF CHURCH GROWTH RELATED TO SPIRITUAL GIFTS, page 25.
____ SOME BASIC IMPLICATIONS OF SPIRITUAL GIFTS, page 22.

Exercises from Section I To Be Done Prior To Class

____ Feedback on 4 Reasons, page 19. Do Questions 1 and 2
____ Feedback on Spiritual Gift and 3 Kinds of Church Growth. Do
Feedback, page 29.

Exercise on Implications To Be Done Prior To Class

____ Read the list of 18 Implications on page 22. From this list
underline 5 which you consider to be very important and for
which you would like clarification in your future study of
spiritual gifts. We will come back to these 5 implications in
later lessons. Right now you are looking at them to
anticipate and motivate for future study.

Follow-Up Exercises On Lesson 1--TO BE DONE AFTER CLASS

____ Gifts Interview With A Full-Time Christian Worker. Use the
Interview Sheet on Lesson 1 page 6. Instructions are given on
the sheet itself.

____ Gifts Identification Sheet. See Lesson 1 page 7. Instructions
are given on the sheet itself.

GIFTS ARE FOR SHARING
by Bobby Clinton

reprinted from Harvest Today April-June 1976

What would you think of a chemist who had never studied chemical theory, a carpenter who couldn't use a hammer, or a tackle on a football team trying to play quarterback? "Ridiculous," you say. Yet these examples are no more absurd than a believer who knows nothing of spiritual gifts, who is not exercising his own gift or, worse, is trying to exercise gifts he doesn't have.

Some believers go through their entire Christian lives without recognizing the importance of spiritual gifts to the church. Some never exercise their gifts or receive the benefit from those who do. And yet the Bible commands, "Serve one another with the particular gifts God has given each of you, as faithful dispensers of the wonderfully varied grace of God."

God's church is an intricate team. He places people according to His game plan in the right positions, each helping and being helped by others on the team in order to contribute to the whole team effort. Each of us fits into God's game plan in a special and specific way. I certainly want to find out how I am supposed to fit, and I believe you do, too. But how do we do it?

Mini-Case Study--Can You Identify the Gifts

A small group of less than 15 people from the Community Bible Church in Miami meets regularly on Tuesday evenings in various homes of its members. The group shares their longings, needs and experiences. In their continuing discovery of the living Christ, they find He meets everyday situations. They study the "one-to-another" commands of the New Testament and how these apply to everyday living. They mutually support each other in attempts to apply given truths in Scripture. Choruses and hymns frequently pop up, catching the spirit of the moment. They pray, mostly conversational, and everyone usually participates. They have developed open relationships in which each member can honestly share strengths and weaknesses because each knows that the group really cares.

Excerpts from A Meeting of the Group

Mary: "Jim, when you explain things like you did about the puzzling passage tonight, I really begin to understand what God means by it. I liked the way you related it to the book as a whole. And I think the principle you saw is right on target for our group."

John: "Well, Mary, I appreciate what you shared with us about your work. I don't see how you can work in that kitchen in the slum area and love those people so much. But I surely admire you. And I know He is changing my own heart attitudes about such people."

Jim: "John, when you shared how God had met your own heart's need through that verse in 2 Corinthians, I can't tell you how encouraging it was to me. I've been going through a similar problem. God has used you to help me face it."

Martha: "I believe God would have this kind of fellowship we enjoy--a vital Christianity--spread to our whole church. I have had a growing conviction about it and believe God is going to do a work of growth in love, unity and in-depth fellowship in our church so that in a year's time our whole church will be alive like we are. I was reading again in John 17 just yesterday morning. I seem to be drawn back to this passage more and more lately. You know the prayer Christ prayed in verse 23? I believe He wants that kind of unity in our church and I am going to trust God for the answer to that prayer. Oh how we need it."

Jerry: "I made another friend at work today! In the most natural way I told him what has been happening in my life lately. He told me he wished he could know God that way. Not only that, but he invited me over to his house this week to explain it in detail. I can hardly wait. Just think. Next week this time he may be a child of God. Pray for me as I speak with him. He may even want to join Roy and me in our noontime Bible study." (Roy made a decision to follow Christ two months ago as a result of Jerry's witness.)

How It Works--Interdependent Ministry

Sally and Richard, a young married couple going through some real financial struggles, explain their situation to the group. All listen intently. Several nod. They understand. Sally and Richard ask for advice. Several share testimonies related to similar experiences and show what God has taught them. Jim briefly summarizes the biblical teaching on guidance, underscoring several principles which most likely apply to the situation.

Then after a good deal of interaction, Dave, the oldest and probably most mature Christian of the group, speaks up. He summarizes what has been said then adds, "It seems to me that God would have you..." and he lists several options. The group concurs, feeling not only that it makes sense, but that this is really God's direction for Sally and Richard. Then they pledge their prayer support and help to the young couple.

This hypothetical situation suggests to me at least two guidelines for identifying spiritual gifts:

First, become involved with a small group of Christians who are practicing reciprocal living as a sharing/caring community.

- It is normal for gifts to emerge and be used in the context of an intimate sharing/caring community.
- It will allow you to exercise your gift though you may not know you have it, possibly because the gift is in the embryonic stage.
- The less publicly-oriented gifts need an occasion which invites their use.
- Practice of reciprocal living in a community encourages the use of gifts.

Second, study the teaching on spiritual gifts in the Scriptures so that you can recognize them in yourself and in others. The passages dealing with spiritual gifts include I Corinthians 12-14; Romans 12:1-8; Ephesians 4:1-16; I Peter 4:7-11. Study these passages yourself and with a good Bible teacher. You may also want to secure one of the many books available on spiritual gifts to aid in your study. In my own book I have gone into detail defining of the gifts and giving practical helps for identifying them.

How Much Do You Already Know About Gifts? Try This Test.

For fun, try the following quiz (answers given at end of article). Based on the small group excerpts and taking for granted the conversations or situations occur frequently, we could assume that:

a) Mary has the gift of _____
b) Jim has the gift of _____
c) Martha has the gift of _____
d) John has the gift of _____
e) Jerry has the gift of _____
f) Dave has the gift of _____

If you had difficulty identifying the individual gifts, then you especially need guideline two, p. 167. Though it is important to identify and develop your gift, the most important part is that you use it. In the context of use, fellow Christians will recognize and confirm your gift. Trying to identify it without exercising it can prove frustrating. But using your gift in the context of a sharing, caring community will make your biblical study of spiritual gifts fruitful and fulfilling. You will be challenged to develop and use your gift to its fullest potential.

Did I communicate at least two main practical guidelines for identifying your gift? Recall in your own words the two guidelines for identifying spiritual gifts presented herein:

Become involved _____
Study _____

Answers to Gifts quiz:

a) mercy b) teaching c) faith d) exhortation e) evangelism f) wisdom

Become involved with a small group of Christians who are practicing reciprocal living as a sharing/caring community.

Study the teaching on spiritual gifts in the Scriptures so that you can recognize them in yourself and in others.

GIFTS INTERVIEW SHEET

NAME OF PERSON INTERVIEWED _____ DATE _____

POSITION OR FUNCTION IN CHURCH _____

INSTRUCTIONS: Explain to the person that you are in a class which is studying spiritual gifts and that you have been given an assignment to interview someone who is a "full-time" Christian worker. Tell the person that you would appreciate help as you seek to learn about spiritual gifts. Please feel free to answer or not answer any of the questions. You give the questions orally and write the answers as they are given. Feel free to ask clarifying questions or any other questions that come to mind as the answer is being given.

1. Have you personally studied the doctrine concerning spiritual gifts? If so, when and in what way (formal class in seminary, church class, personal Bible study, seminar, etc.)

2. Have you personally identified your own spiritual gift(s)? If so, would you please share with me what you feel are your spiritual gifts?

3. What spiritual gifts do you feel our church manifests in abundance?

4. What spiritual gifts do you feel our church does not manifest but needs?

5. What is our church's general view toward Spiritual Gifts? Is there policy I should be aware of?

6. Does our church provide special help for those who want to develop certain spiritual gifts? How or in what way do they do so?

7. What resources would you recommend for one who was interested in studying about spiritual gifts?

8. What reasons could you give for the importance of spiritual gifts to the church?

9. What reasons would you suggest why a believer should know personally about spiritual gifts?

_____
Reflection: This section is to be filled out by you after reflecting on answers to the above questions.

10. What have you learned through this interview?

11. What questions come to mind that you feel need further research? Perhaps you can suggest how to go about getting answers. Or perhaps your class members can give suggestions.

GIFTS IDENTIFICATION SHEET

NAME OF PERSON INTERVIEWED _____ DATE _____

INSTRUCTIONS: Explain to the person that you are in a class which is studying
spiritual gifts and that you have been given an assignment to interview
someone who has been a Christian for several years. Tell the person that you
would appreciate help as you seek to learn about spiritual gifts. Please feel
free to answer or not answer any of the questions. You give the questions
orally and write the answers as they are given. Feel free to ask clarifying
questions or any other questions that come to mind as the answer is being
given. For this questionnaire you will find that many older Christians are
not familiar with definitions of spiritual gifts. They may not be able to
answer some of these questions. Don't embarrass them. If they don't have an
answer to a question--don't press them just move on to the next questions.
One thing you'll probably learn in using this questionnaire is that there is a
great need among older Christians to sharpen their knowledge on the doctrine
of spiritual gifts. Also some Christians may use another name for a given
gift. If they do just scratch out the name given here and use the one they
give you.

1. Which of the following gifts have you observed in a local church?

____ a. apostleship	____ h. gifts of healing	____ o. evangelism
____ b. prophecy	____ i. discerning of spirits	____ p. giving
____ c. teaching	____ j. kinds of tongues	____ q. mercy
____ d. word of wisdom	____ k. interpretation of tongues	____ r. leadership
____ e. word of knowledge	____ l. helps	ruling
____ f. faith	____ m. supportive leadership	____ s. exhortation
____ g. miracles (power)	governments	
	____ n. pastor	

2. If some of these gifts are presently being used in our own church, could
you give me the name of someone who exercises the gift? I would like to talk
to them about their gift: how they discovered they had it, the opportunity
they have had for using it, any lessons they would like to pass along
concerning the gift, etc. I would appreciate any names that you could supply
for any of the gifts listed:

Name of Gift   Person You Personally Feel Has The Gift

____ a. apostleship
____ b. prophecy
____ c. teaching
____ d. word of wisdom
____ e. word of knowledge
____ f. faith
____ g. miracles (power)
____ h. gifts of healing
____ i. discerning of spirits
____ j. kinds of tongues
____ k. interpretation of tongues
____ l. helps

GIFTS IDENTIFICATION SHEET Continued

<u>Name of Gift</u>   <u>Person You Feel Has The Gift</u>

___ m. supportive leadership--governments
___ n. leadership--pastor
___ o. giving
___ p. mercy
___ q. leadership--ruling
___ r. exhortation

3. Choose 1 or 2 of the people given in answer to question 2 above. Contact
them by phone or visit and ask them some of the following questions. Explain
that you are in a spiritual gifts class and are doing an assignment which
involves identifying people's spiritual gift. Explain that someone has said
that they feel they have the gift of _____ and would they answer some
questions concerning this.

   a. Do they agree that yes, they do have that gift?

   b. If not, what gifts do they feel they do have? (If there is a
      negative turn off to either a. or b. just politely thank them for
      their help and disregard the rest of these questions.)

   c. When did you suspect that you had this gift? How did you find out?

   d. In what ways have you been able to use it?

   e. Have you done anything that has helped you develop the gift? If so,
      what?

   f. What advice could you give to someone who believes he has this same
      gift?

_____
Reflection: This section is to be filled out by you after reflecting on
answers to the above questions.

4. What have you learned through this interview?

5. What questions come to mind that you feel need further research? Perhaps
you can suggest how to go about getting answers. Or perhaps your class
members can give suggestions.

THOUGHT QUESTIONS FOR LESSON 1

instructions   Do these thought questions after you have finished your preparation for class. Your study leader will probably use some of the questions to stimulate group discussion during class time.

Thought   Here are some questions to stimulate class discussion:
Questions

1. As a result of your study of lesson 1 what are you personally hoping that God will do for you in this course on spiritual gifts?

2. What Christian person do you admire as an outstanding example of someone who uses his/her spiritual gifts for the benefit of others? Would you describe the way the gift is used and how you see it benefitting others?

3. Of the 3 kinds of church growth described in lesson 1 our church is probably strongest in _____? We probably need the most help in _____?

Questions   Why don't you list some questions of your own which you would
you   like answered concerning spiritual gifts:
have
   1.

   2.

   3.

   4.

LESSON 2. USE HOLY CAUTION IN YOUR STUDY

introduction   The doctrine of spiritual gifts is not without controversy. This lesson points out some of the problems concerning spiritual gifts. It gives some guidelines which will be helpful to you as you study spiritual gifts. But above all you must trust the Holy Spirit to teach you this important doctrine. For it is the Holy Spirit who is at the very heart of this doctrine.

purpose   The purpose of this lesson is to alert you to some of the problems associated with spiritual gifts. As a result of your study of this lesson you should not fear the study of spiritual gifts but will approach it with a proper caution.

objectives   Here is what you should expect to accomplish:

- From the problems described you will list the two which have concerned you in your Christian experience and explain in your own words how and why they have concerned you.

- Given,

    - a list of problems,
    - a list of guidelines,
    - a list of symptomatic statements reflecting problems,

    you should be able to match problems to statements and match guidelines to statements.

- Given a mixed list of characteristic statements or phrases which relate to either the gifts of the Spirit or fruit of the Spirit you will be able to separate the list into the two categories by underlining those statements or phrases which characterize the Fruit of the Spirit.

- Concerning the reception of the gifts of the Spirit you will be able to list the various views as to how and when gifts are received.

choice of assignments   Where time is limited you can expect your group study leader to select assignments from the list which follows. Where adequate time is available you should do all of the assignments. Check with your group study leader on just which assignments you should do.

pre-study assignment   Read the mini-case on Lesson 2 page 3 which points out one of the problems associated with spiritual gifts.

ASSIGNMENT CHECK-OFF LIST FOR LESSON 2

instructions Below are the possible assignments for lesson 2. Do the ones
assigned by your group leader.

Motivation Exercise To Be Done Before Other Assignments

____ Read the Mini-Case study, "Which Way Indicates Unity of the
Spirit?" (Lesson 2 page 3) This excerpt based on the
author's real life experience poses a major problem that
arises concerning gifts.

Reading From Section I To Be Done Prior To Class

____ SOME PROBLEMS AND SOME PRINCIPLES WITH SPIRITUAL GIFTS.
Section I, page 16.

____ DISTINCTION BETWEEN GIFTS AND FRUIT OF THE SPIRIT. Section
I, page 18.

____ HOW ONE RECEIVES SPIRITUAL GIFTS. Section I, page 24.

Exercises From Section I To Be Done Prior To Class

____ Feedback on Fruit and Problems, Section I, pages 19-21
questions 3, 4, 5, 6. (You did questions 1 and 2 in lesson
1).

Follow-Up Exercise on Lesson 1—TO BE DONE AFTER CLASS

____ Problems Interview Sheet. See Lesson 2 page 4.

WHICH WAY INDICATES UNITY OF THE SPIRIT

Bobby was sad. Today was Pastor Jones' farewell sermon. He thought back over the past year and a half. He remembered in this very church sanctuary he had gone forward and rededicated his life to Christ at an invitation Pastor Jones had given. He knew he owed much of his spiritual growth to the many efforts on his behalf by Pastor Jones. He saw Marian, the pastor's wife, sitting near the front of the church. What a sweet Christian she was! He knew he would miss them both. Why did they have to leave? What was the gift of tongues anyway? There to the left was Brother Smith. He was a full-time Christian worker in the state association of the denomination. And there was Brother Thompson, also a high-up executive in the denomination. Both were also local members of this church. Bobby knew that it was at their insistence and pressure that the Jones were asked to resign.

In the sermon Brother Jones shared his testimony of what had happened to him. He had zealously served the Lord for 6 years in this church from its very inception. He had witnessed to many, seen many saved and had seen the church grow over these 6 years until it was the largest (though still only around 250) church the denomination had in this northern state. During the last 6 months, Pastor Jones had felt that his ministry had plateaued. He just didn't seem to be making progress. He had been invited to a Bible study with 6 or 7 other ministers, 4 of whom were of the same denomination. The leader of the study was from a charismatic church. They studied the book of Acts. In the weekly meetings the various passages of Acts were explored. The amazing miracles of the Holy Spirit stood out. Pastor Jones wished he could see that kind of power in his own ministry. Finally after about 2 months of lively Bible Study in Acts, Pastor Jones felt God would give him that kind of power. The group laid hands on him and prayed that God's Spirit would fall upon him. Pastor Jones shared the tremendous excitement and feelings he had as God visited him with the Holy Spirit. He spoke in tongues. For the two months since, Pastor Jones said that he had known God's power in his ministry as never before. He had prayed for the sick and seen God heal people. He had witnessed to people with power and seen them come under deep conviction and come to the Lord. He closed his sermon by saying that he had been asked by several in the church to resign since this experience he had gone through was not in accord with denominational belief and policy. He had offered his resignation since he did not want to stay in a church which would be divided. He said that he planned to start a new church in the same town. It would hold to all the traditional beliefs of the denomination but would also allow the charismatic gifts. His sermon was powerfully given. Bobby looked around the church and saw that many agreed with what they had heard. But others did not. He knew that just about half of the church would follow Pastor Jones and help him start the new church. About half would stay and pick up the pieces.

Bobby pondered over what to do. He knew he did not know what the Bible said about tongues. He did know that it was in the Scriptures. He wasn't sure where. He knew that the denominational leaders who were members of this local church were trained men. They had gone to seminary. They must have some good reasons for forcing Pastor Jones to resign. Who was right? What was the Christian thing to do? Bobby listed the options. He could go with Pastor Jones, but he was a bit frightened about this thing called tongues. He could stay with the traditional church, but he knew it wouldn't be the same without Pastor Jones and Marian. Maybe he should chuck the whole thing and drop out altogether. If the Holy Spirit was real why did this have to happen?

PROBLEMS INTERVIEW SHEET

NAME OF PERSON INTERVIEWED _____ DATE _____

instructions   Explain to the person you will interview that you are taking a
course on spiritual gifts. Explain also that you are interested
in understanding some of the controversial points about this
important doctrine. Orally give the following questions and
write down a summary of the answers given you.

1. Would you please give your own view of the distinction between the fruit of
the Spirit and the gifts of the Spirit. I am particularly interested in your
view concerning whether gifts are to be used as a sign of a Spirit-dominated
life or whether the fruit of the Spirit manifests the presence of the Holy
Spirit or whether it is some combination of the two.

2. In your opinion, when are spiritual gifts given and how are they given?

3. In your opinion, what are the problems, if any, that you feel are
associated with spiritual gifts? What cautions would you give a person who is
beginning to study this doctrine?

4. Here are some guidelines that we have studied in our class on spiritual
gifts (see Lesson 2, page 5 for summarized guidelines). Would you glance at
these and point out which ones you agree with or disagree with or in what way
you would word them? Or, if you have your own guidelines would you share them
with me. (Note on the Guidelines Sheet any pertinent comments.)

SOME GUIDELINES TO REMEMBER IN YOUR STUDY OF SPIRITUAL GIFTS

No.	Label	STATEMENT	EXPLANATION
1	dis-agreement	BE TOLERANT AND ALLOW OTHERS THEIR VIEWS.	Disagreements usually indicate the lack of Biblical evidence upon which to resolve the question. Otherwise, all would have the same clear answer .
2	spiritual or natural?	USE GIFTS OR NATURAL ABILITIES WHETHER OR NOT YOU CAN TELL THE DIFFERENCE.	Don't worry about distinctions between gifts and natural abilities but make sure that you use both in service for God. He will clarify any necessary distinctions. Some call certain abilities natural gifts. Others call them spiritual gifts. The main focus should be on using what God has given, not on identifying it.
3	neglect	WHEN INTRODUCING CHANGE CONCERNING NEGLECT OF GIFTS MAINTAIN UNITY. GO AT THE PACE OF THE GROUP AND BUILD ON PAST EXPERIENCE.	People who are not used to the idea of spiritual gifts may resist attempts to introduce it in the church. Slowly introduce the idea. First model it by using your own gift to serve others. Don't imply that previous ministry was wrong because of a lack of emphasis on gifts. Recognize the ways in which gifts have already been used in your past situation. Build on that.
4	abuse 1	DON'T OVERSTRESS CERTAIN GIFTS AS BEING THE IM-PORTANT ONE(S) THAT ALL SHOULD HAVE.	Beware of stressing improper balance of any gifts to the exclusion or belittling of other gifts. Strong leaders usually project their own dominant gift on members of their churches. This can cause people to feel guilty if they don't have the same gift. A body will have need of all kinds of gifts.
5	abuse 2	GIFTS ARE FOR SERVICE AND NOT SIGNS OF SPIRITUALITY.	Distinguish between exercise of gifts in the body (encourage this) and using a gift as a sign of spirituality (discourage this).
6	abuse 3	BOTH FRUIT AND GIFTS ARE VITAL. NEITHER REPLACES THE OTHER.	Know the difference between the fruit of the Spirit and the gifts of the Spirit. Fruit indicates spiritual maturity. Gifts do not. They are for service.

OVERALL
- SPIRITUAL GIFTS MUST NOT BE IGNORED SIMPLY BECAUSE THERE ARE PROBLEMS ASSOCIATED WITH THEM.
- TRUST THE HOLY SPIRIT TO GIVE CLARITY IN ORDER THAT YOUR CHURCH MAY FUNCTION INTERDEPENDENTLY AS A GIFTED BODY.

SUMMARY OF UNIT 1

introduction   You have now studied the first two lessons on spiritual gifts.
These lessons are lessons that are intended to give you a
balanced perspective as you approach your study of spiritual
gifts.

REVIEW   In lesson 1 we have
OF MAJOR
TEACHING   ● defined the concept of spiritual gifts,
POINTS
               ● related gifts to 3 kinds of church growth (qualitative,
                 quantitative, organic),

               ● listed some reasons why gifts are important to you and to
                 the church,

               ● seen some implications of spiritual gifts for the church.

               In addition, in lesson 2 we have

               ● pointed out some of the problems involved with the study
                 of spiritual gifts,

               ● talked about how one gets a spiritual gift.

REVIEW OF   We have also learned from the experiences of others. We have,
EXPERIENTIAL
LEARNING   ● interviewed a full-time Christian worker concerning that
                 person's view of gifts,

               ● interviewed a worker concerning problems that worker has
                 seen concerning spiritual gifts.

LOOKING   In the next several lessons you will be examining the major
AHEAD   Biblical material on spiritual gifts. There are 4 passages that
               mention spiritual gifts in the context. We will look at each of
               them individually. The lists of gifts that we see in the
               various passages are not the same. There is some overlap of
               names of gifts but no passage has a comprehensive list.
               Finally, we will compare all of the passages and arrive at the
               names of the gifts we will study. You will find that different
               authors writing on spiritual gifts will have different names for
               gifts than I use and may also have different numbers of gifts.
               You will remember my cautionary guideline: where there is much
               difference, probably the Scriptures are not totally clear on the
               issue, so be tolerant.

LESSON 3. CONFUSION AT CORINTH

introduction This is the first of 4 lessons which studies the Bible material relating to spiritual gifts. There are 4 basic passages which treat spiritual gifts. They are

- I Corinthians 12-14
- Romans 12:1-8
- Ephesians 4:1-16
- I Peter 4:10,11

None of these passages were given in the Scriptures to define and exhaustively treat the doctrine of spiritual gifts. Each was given in the context of some other subject. Therefore we must be careful and interpret each of these passages in the light of their original purpose. And in doing this we will also be able to learn what we can about spiritual gifts.

purpose This lesson on spiritual gifts taken from I Corinthians will point out to you the basic guideline about over emphasizing one gift to the exclusion or belittling of others. It will also emphasize the necessity of the doctrine of spiritual gifts to the essential nature of the church.

objectives When you finish this lesson you will have,

o listed the spiritual gifts mentioned in I Cor 12-14,
o described the problem that Paul was trying to solve,
o read the summarized flow of Paul's argument so that you know the context in which the verses on gifts fit,
o personally recognized something of the controversial nature that Paul was dealing with.

choice of Where time is limited you can expect your group study leader to
assignments select assignments from the list which follows. Where adequate time is available you should do all of the assignments. Check with your group study leader on just which assignments you should do.

ASSIGNMENT CHECK-OFF LIST

instructions Below are the possible assignments for lesson 3. Do the ones
assigned by your group leader.

READING FROM THE BIBLE To Be Done Before Reading From Section II

___ Read I Corinthians 12-14 in the Bible of your choice.

EXERCISE TO DO WHILE YOU ARE READING I CORINTHIANS 12-14

___ Compile a List of gifts mentioned in this passage. Later we
will compile a list for each Bible passage studied. We will
then be able to compare the lists. Later we will also define
each of these gifts.

READING FROM SECTION II

___ Read the Summary of Gifts Passage—I Corinthians 12-14, Section
II, page 38.

___ Compare your list of gifts with the list given on page 40.

___ Note the basic problem Paul was seeking to solve.

___ Read carefully Paul's answer to the problem. You will see that
I break I Corinthians 12 into three major sections. There are
two major teaching points in the first two sections and three
major teaching points in the 4th section. I summarize chapter
13 into 2 major points and chapter 14 into 3 major points.

Follow-Up Exercise on Lesson 3—TO BE DONE AFTER CLASS

___ Unique Gifts in Corinthians—Interview (see Lesson 3 page 3)

ANSWER THE FOLLOWING QUESTIONS

1. From your list of gifts give here the ones which Paul says are valid
only for the early church.

2. Which gift according to Paul is the test of true spirituality?

3. When Paul contrasts the gift of prophecy (explained in I Cor. chapter
14) with the gift of tongues he is pointing out:
___a. that tongues is more valuable than prophecy
___b. tongues and prophecy are equally valuable
___c. a principle that the relative value of spiritual gifts is to be
tested by their usefulness to the church as a whole.
___d. none of the above

UNIQUE GIFTS IN CORINTHIANS--INTERVIEW SHEET

_____ word of Wisdom	_____ miracles (power)	_____ kinds of tongues
_____ word of Knowledge	_____ gifts of healing	_____ interpretation of tongues
_____ faith	_____ discerning of spirits	_____ helps
		_____ governments

introduction   These gifts occur only in Corinthians. Some will say that they do not exist today. Others not only disagree but claim to use them. This exercise challenges these two views. PART A lets you talk with someone who does not believe that these gifts (or at least some of them) exist. PART B will allow you to talk with someone who does believe that these gifts exist and in fact claims to have and use one or more of these gifts. Your group leader will help you select people to interview.

PART A   NAME OF PERSON INTERVIEWED _____ Date _____

instructions   Tell the person you are interviewing that you are studying spiritual gifts in I Corinthians. Your instructor has informed you that some people do not believe that the unique gifts listed above are present in the church today. Would he/she be able to answer some questions to help you understand their view. Put your answers on separate sheets of paper and bring them to class. Be prepared to share what you have learned.

1. Glance over the list of gifts unique to I Corinthians 12. Which of these gifts do you feel are not in existence in the church today?
2. Why do you feel that these gifts are not in existence today?
3. Other people feel these gifts do exist today. They claim to have and use these gifts. How do you explain this if your view of them not being in existence is true?
4. At least three other gifts besides the ones listed above are given in I Corinthians 12. These are apostleship, prophecy, and teaching. Do you feel that these gifts are also non-existent in the church today?

PART B   NAME OF PERSON INTERVIEWED _____ Date _____

instructions   Inform this person you are learning about spiritual gifts and have some questions concerning the present day manifestation and use of these gifts, particularly those listed above.

1. Are any of these gifts used in your own church? Mark with a C any which the person has seen used in conjunction with the church's activities.
2. Do you personally possess any of these gifts? Mark with a P any possessed by the person you are interviewing.
3. Explain how these gifts are used in the church and how they benefit the church. Have the person give some actual illustrations of how the gifts are manifested and used?
4. Optional: You will learn more from actually attending a church activity in which these gifts are used. Jot down your observations. Feel free to question people at such an activity and learn what you can.

LESSON 4. REACHING OUT FROM ROME

introduction   This is the second of 4 lessons which studies the Bible material relating to spiritual gifts. There are 4 basic passages which treat spiritual gifts. They are

- I Corinthians 12-14
- Romans 12:1-8
- Ephesians 4:1-16
- I Peter 4:10,11

None of these passages were given in the Scriptures to define and exhaustively treat the doctrine of spiritual gifts. Each was given in the context of some other subject. Therefore we must be careful and interpret each of these passages in the light of their original purpose. And in doing this we will also be able to learn what we can about spiritual gifts.

purpose   This lesson on spiritual gifts taken from Romans is given to motivate the Roman believers to reach their full potential. This involves commitment (Romans 12:1,2). But it also requires evaluation of individual potential. People are to evaluate themselves and then live up to the potential that they have. This includes using their gifts "according to the measure of faith" that God has given them. Remember, Romans is a missionary book. Paul is seeking to expand the horizons of the Roman church. Whereas in Corinthians Paul is dealing with a problem involved with spiritual gifts here in Romans there is not a problem but simply an exhortation to learn and grow concerning spiritual gifts.

objectives   When you finish this lesson you will have,

- listed the spiritual gifts mentioned in Romans,
- read the summarized flow of Paul's argument so that you know the context in which the verses on gifts fit,
- personally recognized something of the value of the gifts which are unique to Romans.

choice of   Where time is limited you can expect your group study leader to
assignments   select assignments from the list which follows. Where adequate time is available you should do all of the assignments. Check with your group study leader on just which assignments you should do.

ASSIGNMENT CHECK-OFF LIST

instructions   Below are the possible assignments for lesson 4. Do the ones
assigned by your group leader.

READING FROM THE BIBLE To Be Done Before Reading From Section II

____ Read Romans 12:1-8 in the Bible of your choice.

EXERCISE TO DO WHILE YOU ARE READING Romans 12:1-8

____ Compile a list of gifts mentioned in this passage. Later we
will compile a list for each Bible passage studied. We will
then be able to compare the lists. Later we will also define
each of these gifts.

READING FROM SECTION II

____ Read the Summary of Gifts Passage--Romans 12:1-8 in Section
II, page 41.

____ Compare your list of gifts with the list given on page 41.

____ Note the basic principles that come from this positive
exhortation to expand and use our potential. See especially
the five listed at the bottom of page 41.

Follow-Up Exercise on Lesson 4—TO BE DONE AFTER CLASS

____ Unique Gifts in Romans--Interview (Lesson 4, page 3)

ANSWER THE FOLLOWING QUESTIONS

1. Which gifts occur in Romans and do not occur in the I Corinthians
passage that you have previously studied? List any you see here.

2. Which gifts occur in both of the gifts passages that you have
studied--I Corinthians and Romans?

UNIQUE GIFTS IN ROMANS--INTERVIEW SHEET

_____ exhortation   _____ mercy
_____ ministering   _____ ruling
_____ giving

introduction   The above named gifts are listed only in Romans. Most people do
               not question whether or not these gifts exist today. They are
               non-controversial gifts. Perhaps that explains why their
               existence is not questioned. The problem with these gifts lies
               rather in their relative obscurity. Few people really know
               about these gifts. And churches do not normally promote
               activities which allow all of these gifts to be used. The focus
               on this interview is to observe just how little is really known
               about these gifts by the average church member and to observe
               what activities are available which will allow individuals to
               use these gifts in the church.

NAME OF PERSON INTERVIEWED _____ Date _____

instructions   Tell the person you are interviewing that you are studying the
               lesser known spiritual gifts which are mentioned in Romans.
               Would he/she answer any of the questions below? Do the
               questions orally and record the answers you hear. If they ask
               you to define any of these gifts just tell them that you have
               not yet studied the definitions but are doing preliminary work
               involving listing the names of gifts and finding out if people
               in the church know about them.

1. Glance over the list of lesser known gifts unique to Romans 12. Which of
    these gifts are you personally familiar with? Mark with an F any gifts
    which are familiar to the person being interviewed.
2. Could you suggest anyone in our church who has any of these gifts? Take
    down the name of any such names suggested along with the gift identified.
3. For any such names given, call the folks up and tell them that someone in
    the church has suggested that they have the spiritual gift of _____
    which is named in Romans 12:1-8. Do they agree with that assessment?
    Could they tell anything about how the gift can be exercised in our
    church? Are there activities which are especially good for the use of
    this gift? How have they seen their gift used to the benefit of the
    church? Do they feel that their gift could be used even more effectively
    if their were other outlets in the church for the gifts to be used. Could
    they suggest some such outlets?
4. Optional: You will sometimes find that churches which stress some of the
    unique gifts we saw in I Corinthians have structures, means, activities,
    and outlets for using those unique gifts since they are emphasized in the
    church. However, many of these churches do not have structures, means,
    activities, and outlets for using the unique gifts of Romans. Why don't
    you use the same three questions above with the person you interviewed in
    Part B of the interview for lesson 3?

LESSON 5. THE BIG PICTURE--EPHESIANS 4

introduction   This is the third of 4 lessons which studies the Bible material
relating to spiritual gifts. There are 4 basic passages which
treat spiritual gifts. They are

- I Corinthians 12-14
- Romans 12:1-8
- Ephesians 4:1-16
- I Peter 4:10,11

None of these passages were given in the Scriptures to define
and exhaustively treat the doctrine of spiritual gifts. Each
was given in the context of some other subject. Therefore, we
must be careful and interpret each of these passages in the
light of their original purpose. And in doing this we will also
be able to learn what we can about spiritual gifts.

purpose   This lesson on spiritual gifts taken from Ephesians is given to
inform us of the big picture, that is, the purpose of Christ
giving gifts to the church worldwide. In Corinthians one local
church is involved, a problematic one at that. In Romans, a
cluster of small churches is dealt with. Individuals in these
local house churches are asked to recognize and use gifts. Now
in Ephesians we see the overall purpose of gifts for all
churches everywhere.

objectives   When you finish this lesson you will have

- listed the spiritual gifts mentioned in Ephesians,
- noted two important overview principles,
- personally recognized something of the value of the leadership
  gifts and the gifts of the body and see the interrelationship
  between them,
- noted possible differences of interpretation of this key
  passage.

choice of   Where time is limited you can expect your group study leader to
assignments   select assignments from the list which follows. Where adequate
time is available you should do all of the assignments. Check
with your group study leader on just which assignments you
should do.

ASSIGNMENT CHECK-OFF LIST

instructions Below are the possible assignments for lesson 5. Do the ones assigned by your group leader.

READING FROM THE BIBLE To Be Done Before Reading From Section II

___ Read Ephesians 4:1-16 in the Bible of your choice.

EXERCISE TO DO WHILE YOU ARE READING Ephesians 4:1-16

___ Compile a list of gifts mentioned in this passage. This will complete our individual listing of gifts from the gifts passage. We are now almost ready to compare the lists. Later we will also define each of these gifts.

READING FROM SECTION II

___ Read the Summary of Gifts Passage—Ephesians 4:1-16 in Section II, page 42.

___ Compare your list of gifts with the list given on page 42.

___ Note the two overview principles that are given in this passage. Note particularly how the leadership gifts are related to the gifts of others in the body.

___ Read especially the block of information that tells of possible difference of interpretation of this passage.

Follow-Up Exercise on Lesson 5—TO BE DONE AFTER CLASS

___ Leadership Interview (Lesson 5, page 3)

ANSWER THE FOLLOWING QUESTIONS

1. Which gifts occur in Ephesians and do not occur in the I Corinthians and Romans passages that you have previously studied? List any you see here.

2. Which gifts occur also in this passage and in the other gifts passages that you have studied—I Corinthians and Romans?

LEADERSHIP INTERVIEW

introduction This is a crucial passage which gives the underlying philosophy of the use of gifts for the church--both the local church and the universal church. You will note that this passage distinguishes clearly between two categories of gifts-- leadership gifts and other gifts. You will have a tendency to identify leadership gifts with what you think of as full-time Christian workers. While it is true that many full-time Christian workers are leaders, in the sense of the passage it is also true that many are not. And many who are not full-time Christian workers do function as those exercising leadership gifts. In this interview you are to establish this fact by interviewing two leaders (a full-time Christian worker who is actually functioning with a leadership gift and a non-full-time worker who is also functioning with a leadership gift). Your class leader will help you select people to interview.

NAME OF FULL-TIME PERSON INTERVIEWED _____ Date _____

instructions Tell the person you are interviewing that you are studying the Ephesians passage on spiritual gifts. Tell that person that he/she has been suggested as a person having one of the leadership gifts listed in Eph 4:11. You would like some opinions on the following questions.

1. There are several opinions on this passage. Most agree that the passage is dealing with spiritual gifts in some way. Would you look at the lists given below? They represent different views of Ephesians 4 in terms of spiritual gifts. Please check the one which is most closely aligned with your own view.

___ List 1   ___ List 2   ___ List 3   ___ List 4   ___ List 5

apostleship	apostleship	evangelism	evangelism	These are not
prophecy	prophecy	pastor	pastor-teacher	gifts but are
evangelism	evangelism	teacher		roles. Some
pastor	pastor-teacher			may no longer
teacher				exist.

2. How does this apply to you personally? That is, where do you see yourself fitting in if this Ephesians passage were to be applied to our church?

3. It would appear that the leaders mentioned in Ephesians 4:11 have a responsibility to equip others in the church to actually do the ministry. In what way do our leaders do this, in your opinion?

NAME OF NON-FULL-TIME PERSON INTERVIEWED _____ Date _____

instructions Repeat the same questions. You will most likely get a different perspective altogether. Be prepared to share what you have seen in talking with these two different types of leaders.

LESSON 6. PUTTING IT TOGETHER--COMPARATIVE STUDY

introduction   This is the final lesson which studies the Bible material relating to spiritual gifts. We have covered the 3 major passages that treat spiritual gifts. We will cover the 4th passage in this lesson as well as do a comparative study on the four passages. Again to refresh your memory here are the 4 passages:

- I Corinthians 12-14
- Romans 12:1-8
- Ephesians 4:1-16
- I Peter 4:10,11

Remember that none of these passages were given in the Scriptures to define and exhaustively treat the doctrine of spiritual gifts. Each was given in the context of some other subject. Therefore we must be careful and interpret each of these passages in the light of their original purpose. And in doing this we will also be able to learn what we can about spiritual gifts.

purpose   This lesson on spiritual gifts will first look at the I Peter 4 passage dealing with gifts. It will then do a comparative study of the listing of gifts for the passages and draw some tentative conclusions on how to categorize gifts. These categories will be used in lessons 7,8,9 when we define each of the gifts.

objectives   When you finish this lesson you will be able to,

- list the 4 passages on gifts in order of amount of information provided on gifts,
- state in your own words the purpose of each of the 4 passages in terms of its contribution to the book in which it occurs,
- identify gifts by name which occur uniquely in each passage,
- identify gifts which occur in more than one passage,
- identify at least one unique principle of truth from each passage,
- write in your own words the two basic emphases about using gifts which occur in all 4 passages.

choice of   You should do all of the assignments for this lesson since it
assignments   is a review lesson covering our study of the listing of spiritual gifts.

ASSIGNMENT CHECK-OFF LIST FOR LESSON 6

instructions Below are the assignments for lesson 6.

READING FROM THE BIBLE To Be Done Before Reading From Section II

___ Read I Peter 4:7-11 in the Bible of your choice.

EXERCISE TO DO WHILE YOU ARE READING I Peter 4:7-11

___ Note the way believers are to use their gifts. There are
several emphases that are highlighted. See if you can identify
them.

READING FROM SECTION II

___ Read the Summary of Gifts Passage—I Peter 4:7-11 in Section
II, page 44.

___ Note especially the principles of truth drawn from I Peter.

___ Study the COMPARATIVE LISTING OF GIFTS FROM 4 PASSAGES in
Section II, page 45.

___ Read the 4 WAYS TO CATEGORIZE GIFTS in Section II, page 46.

___ Read the HOW GIFTS AND KINDS OF GROWTH ARE RELATED in Section
II, page 47.

Review Exercise on Lesson 6—TO BE DONE BEFORE COMING TO CLASS

___ Do the Feedback On Correlating The Gifts Passages in Section II
page 48.

SUMMARY OF UNIT 2

introduction In Unit 2 you have read through the Biblical Material on Spiritual gifts. You have seen the material in terms of the context in which it was written.

REVIEW
OF MAJOR
TEACHING
POINTS

In lessons 3, 4, 5, and 6 we,

- listed the spiritual gifts we saw in each passage,

- studied why the author actually wrote the passage, that is, what he was trying to do in the passage,

- identified the spiritual gifts which were unique to each passage,

- noted the two overview principles (love, service) that occur in connection with all of the major passages.

REVIEW OF
EXPERIENTIAL
LEARNING

We have also learned from the experiences of others. We have

- interviewed two different Christians with differing views on the gifts listed in 1st Corinthians,

- interviewed a worker having one of the unique gifts mentioned in the Romans passage,

- talked to 2 different kinds of leaders in connection with the teachings of the Ephesian passage.

LOOKING
AHEAD

In the next several lessons you will be studying the definitions of gifts that I have arrived at in my Bible study of the major Biblical material on spiritual gifts. I will also point out to you implications of the various definitions. I will suggest symptoms that may be seen in people who have these gifts. I will mention how these gifts can be used. You will recognize that my list of gifts sticks close to gifts actually mentioned in the gifts passages. Other people are more open-ended than I concerning gifts. They list many other gifts and use other passages to support their reasoning. I recognize that none of the passages give a comprehensive list of gifts. The fact that each passage lists some gifts not seen in other passages suggests that there may be more gifts than are actually listed in the major passages. I am open to this but feel bound only to define those that I know are gifts. Certainly the more important gifts will be listed in these major passages. Be thinking as you study each definition: "Do I know someone who has that gift?" "Is it possible that I may have this gift?"

LESSON 7. MATURITY GROWTH GIFTS

introduction   This is the first of 3 lessons which defines the spiritual
gifts.   Thus far, we have listed a number of gifts which
occurred in the major passages on gifts. We sought to compare
what we saw in the passages and identified gifts which were
common in the passages and gifts which were unique to each
passage. We categorized the gifts into three major categories:

- GIFTS HAVING A PRIMARY FOCUS TOWARD MATURITY CHURCH
  GROWTH, NUMERICAL CHURCH GROWTH, AND ORGANIC CHURCH
  GROWTH,
- HOW BEST EXERCISED IN TERMS OF GATHERED CHURCH, DISPERSED
  CHURCH, BOTH, OR REGIONAL CHURCH,
- IN TERMS OF LEADERSHIP GIFTS AND SUPPORTIVE GIFTS.

Now we will use the first category listed above for the next 3
lessons. This lesson will look at gifts which have a primary
focus toward maturity growth.

purpose   This lesson will define the maturity church growth gifts.

objectives   By the time you finish this lesson you should be able to,
- match the name of a gift with its definition or key
  word(s) from its definition,
- match a gift with its symptoms,
- match a gift with its primary uses,
- match a gift with a contextual description of it,
- match a gift with a Scriptural passage related to it.

assignments   You will need to do all of this lesson.

ASSIGNMENT CHECK-OFF LIST FOR LESSON 7

instructions   Below are the assignments for lesson 7. Notice particularly the assignment associated with the CHECKLIST TO FOLLOW IN IDENTIFYING YOUR SPIRITUAL GIFT. You will be continuing to update this checklist in the next several lessons.

READING FROM THE BIBLE

____ There is no special assignment for reading the Bible. You may desire to look up various passages which are mentioned in the definition of each gift.

READING FROM SECTION II

____ Review the following pages from Section II
4 WAYS TO CATEGORIZE GIFTS (page 46)
HOW GIFTS AND KINDS OF GROWTH ARE INTERRELATED (page 47)
____ Read OVERALL PROCEDURE FOR ARRIVING AT DEFINITIONS OF SPIRITUAL GIFTS (page 50)
____ Read GIFTS FOCUSED ON MATURITY CHURCH GROWTH (page 51)
____ Read PROPHECY (page 52,53)
____ Read TEACHING (page 54-56)
____ Read PASTORING (page 57-59)
____ Read WORD OF KNOWLEDGE, WORD OF WISDOM (page 60-62)
____ Read EXHORTATION (page 63,64)
____ Read TONGUES, INTERPRETATION OF TONGUES (page 65,66)
____ Read DISCERNMENT (page 67,68)
____ Read FAITH (page 69,70)
____ Read GIVING (page 71,72)

EXERCISES TO BE DONE BEFORE CLASS

____ Do Feedback on Maturity Gifts (page 73)
____ Fill in as much as you can of the CHECKLIST TO FOLLOW IN IDENTIFYING YOUR SPIRITUAL GIFT on page 35. You have studied 11 gifts so far. See how many of the various blanks you can fill in. Particularly seek to identify some of these gifts in people who are in your own church (final column—Seen this gift in some person I am acquainted with)

FOLLOW-UP EXERCISE ON LESSON 7—TO BE DONE AFTER CLASS

____ Choose any gift that you have studied. Identify someone with that gift. Talk with that person about the following:

● When did it become evident to the person that God had definitely given the gift?
● How has knowing that the gift was from God influenced priorities?
● In what ways is the gift exercised? That is, in small groups, large groups, individually, privately, etc.?
● What has the person done to grow in the use of the gift?

LESSON 8   NUMERICAL CHURCH GROWTH GIFTS

introduction   This is the second of three lessons which defines the spiritual
gifts. Thus far, we have listed a number of gifts which
occurred in the major passages on gifts. We have used the major
category which looks at gifts in terms of their focus toward
MATURITY, NUMERICAL, and ORGANIC church growth. In the last
lesson we studied the MATURITY CHURCH GROWTH GIFTS. In this
lesson we will look at the NUMERICAL CHURCH GROWTH GIFTS.

purpose   This lesson will define the numerical church growth gifts.

objectives   By the time you finish this lesson you should be able to,

- match the name of a gift with its definition or key word(s) from its definition,

- match a gift with its symptoms,

- match a gift with its primary uses,

- match a gift with a contextual description of it,

- match a gift with a Scriptural passage related to it.

assignments   You will need to do all of this lesson.

ASSIGNMENT CHECK-OFF LIST FOR LESSON 8

instructions   Below are the assignments for lesson 8. Notice particularly the
assignment associated with the CHECKLIST TO FOLLOW IN
IDENTIFYING YOUR SPIRITUAL GIFT. You will be continuing to
update this checklist in the next several lessons.

READING FROM THE BIBLE

___ There is no special assignment for reading the Bible. You may
desire to look up various passages which are mentioned in the
definition of each gift.

READING FROM SECTION II

___ HOW GIFTS AND KINDS OF GROWTH ARE INTERRELATED (page 47)
___ Read GIFTS FOCUSED ON NUMERICAL CHURCH GROWTH (page 74)
___ Read APOSTLESHIP (page 75-77)
___ Read EVANGELISM (page 78-80)
___ Read MIRACLES (page 81)
___ Read HEALING (page 82,83)
___ Read MERCY (page 84,85)

EXERCISES TO BE DONE BEFORE CLASS

___ Do Feedback on Numerical Gifts (page 86)
___ Again, fill in as much as you can of the CHECKLIST TO FOLLOW IN
IDENTIFYING YOUR SPIRITUAL GIFT on page 35.   You have studied
16 gifts so far. See how many of the various blanks you can
fill in. Particularly seek to identify some of these gifts in
people who are in your own church (final column—Seen this gift
in some person I am acquainted with)

FOLLOW-UP EXERCISE ON LESSON 8—TO BE DONE AFTER CLASS

___ Choose any one of these gifts that you have studied. Identify
someone in your church who has this gift. Talk with that person
about the following:

● When did it become evident to the person that God had
definitely given the gift?
● How has knowing that the gift was from God influenced
priorities?
● In what ways is the gift exercised? That is, in small groups,
large groups, individually, privately, etc.?
● What has the person done to develop and grow in the use of the
gift?

Be sure you record your observations of your talk with the
person concerning the above questions. Come prepared to share
with the class what you have learned.

LESSON 9   ORGANIC CHURCH GROWTH GIFTS

introduction   This is the final lesson defining the spiritual gifts. Thus
far, we have listed a number of gifts which occurred in the
major passages on gifts. We have used the major category which
looks at gifts in terms of their focus toward MATURITY,
NUMERICAL, and ORGANIC church growth. In the previous lessons
we studied the MATURITY CHURCH GROWTH GIFTS and the NUMERICAL
CHURCH GROWTH GIFTS. In this lesson we will look at the ORGANIC
CHURCH GROWTH GIFTS.

purpose   This lesson will define the organic church growth gifts.

objectives   By the time you finish this lesson you should be able to

● match the name of a gift with its definition or key
  word(s) from its definition,

● match a gift with its symptoms,

● match a gift with its primary uses,

● match a gift with a contextual description of it,

● match a gift with a Scriptural passage related to it.

assignments   You will need to do all of this lesson.

optional   You have now studied all of the definitions of the gifts. You
may wish to go back to lesson 1 and review the article "Gifts
Are For Sharing." Now you should be able to identify the gifts
that are manifest in it.

optional   By this time you should be well-acquainted with the members of
your spiritual gifts class. Why don't you try to put them on
your CHECKOFF LIST, page 35.

ASSIGNMENT CHECK-OFF LIST FOR LESSON 9

instructions   Below are the assignments for lesson 9. Notice particularly the
assignment associated with the CHECKLIST TO FOLLOW IN
IDENTIFYING YOUR SPIRITUAL GIFT. You will be continuing to
update this checklist in the next several lessons.

READING FROM THE BIBLE

____ There is no special assignment for reading the Bible. You may
desire to look up various passages which are mentioned in the
definition of each gift.

READING FROM SECTION II

____ HOW GIFTS AND KINDS OF GROWTH ARE INTERRELATED (page 47)
____ Read GIFTS FOCUSED ON ORGANIC CHURCH GROWTH (page 87)
____ Read GOVERNMENTS (page 88,89)
____ Read HELPS (page 90,91)

EXERCISES TO BE DONE BEFORE CLASS

____ Do Feedback on Organic Gifts (page 92)
____ Again, fill in as much as you can of the CHECKLIST TO FOLLOW IN
IDENTIFYING YOUR SPIRITUAL GIFT on page 35. You have studied 16
gifts so far. See how many of the various blanks you can fill
in. Particularly seek to identify some of these gifts in people
who are in your own church (final column—Seen this gift in some
person I am acquainted with)
____ Do the Feedback on all the Gifts (page 93-95)

FOLLOW-UP EXERCISE ON LESSON 9—TO BE DONE AFTER CLASS

____ Choose any one of these gifts that you have studied. Identify
someone in your church who has this gift. Talk with that person
about the following:

● When did it become evident to the person that God had
definitely given the gift?
● How has knowing that the gift was from God influenced
priorities?
● In what ways is the gift exercised? That is, in small groups,
large groups, individually, privately, etc.?
● What has the person done to develop and grow in the use of the
gift?

Be sure you record your observations of your talk with the
person concerning the above questions. Come prepared to share
with the class what you have learned.

SUMMARY OF UNIT 3

introduction   In Unit 3 you have studied lessons 7, 8, and 9. These lessons
               defined my list of gifts by breaking them up into three
               categories: numerical church growth gifts, maturity church
               growth gifts, and organic church growth gifts.

REVIEW   In lessons 7, 8, and 9 we,
OF MAJOR
TEACHING   ● defined each gift,
POINTS
                   ● gave implications concerning each gift,

                   ● gave symptomatic indicators for each gift,

                   ● suggested uses for the various gifts.

REVIEW OF   We have also learned from the experiences of others. We have,
EXPERIENTIAL
LEARNING   ● talked to people who have these gifts and learned what we
                     could about when they knew they had the gift, how they
                     use it, how they have developed it, etc.

LOOKING   In the next several lessons you will be using what you have
AHEAD   learned about these gifts as you seek to identify the gift or
               gifts that you have. You will analyze yourself in several ways
               to see what you can learn about your own spiritual gift. You
               will also get others to tell you what they have seen about you
               and your spiritual gift. You will also try to identify the
               gifts of others.

LESSON 10   MY VIEW OF MY GIFT(S)

introduction   In Section I, I gave 4 steps suggesting How You Profit from Teaching on Spiritual Gifts. Those 4 steps included,

1. IDENTIFY YOUR GIFT.
2. SET OUT A SPECIFIC PLAN TO DEVELOP YOUR GIFT.
3. CHOOSE YOUR SERVICE IN TERMS OF YOUR GIFT.
4. USE YOUR GIFT.

In this lesson and the two to follow we will be expanding on step 1 given above. In fact we will be following the basic ideas given on page 37 which tells HOW TO IDENTIFY YOUR GIFT. We have already been following the suggested procedures as we worked through the last several lessons. You will remember that those lessons studied the definitions of the gifts. It is an exciting thing to realize that God has gifted you with a spiritual gift or gifts which He wants you to use with others in the body of Christ. It is even more exciting to actually use your gift with others so that they benefit. And the next several lessons will help us begin to do just that—to identify and use our gifts in ministering to others.

purpose   Lesson 10 focuses on STEP 2 of HOW TO IDENTIFY YOUR GIFT.

STEP 2. ANALYZE YOURSELF FOR BACKGROUND INFORMATION THAT MAY CORRELATE WITH YOUR GIFT.

objectives   Here is what you will have accomplished by the time you finish Lesson 10. You will have,

● listed one or more gifts that are suggested by the "Gifts Correlated To Traits Table,"

● recognized the 5 principles underlying the "Inward Conviction Questionnaire" so that you can tell if any of the 5 actually apply to your own personal situation,

● listed one or more gifts that are suggested by the "Inward Conviction Questionnaire,"

● listed one or more gifts that are suggested by the "Experience Questionnaire."

● reviewed the definitions of any gifts indicated from using the various Questionnaires.

choice
of
assignments   Where time is limited you can expect your group leader to select assignments from the list which follows. Where adequate time is available you should do all of the assignments. I would recommend the 3 exercises you shall do in order of importance in this sequence: Inward Conviction Questionnaire, Experience Questionnaire, Gifts Correlated to Traits Questionnaire.

ASSIGNMENT CHECK-OFF LIST FOR LESSON 10

instructions   Below are the possible assignments for lesson 10. Do the ones
assigned by your group leader.

READING FROM SECTION I TO BE DONE PRIOR TO QUESTIONNAIRES

____ Read page 28, HOW TO INSURE THAT YOU WILL PROFIT FROM TEACHING
ON SPIRITUAL GIFTS.

READING FROM SECTION II TO BE DONE PRIOR TO QUESTIONNAIRES

____ Read page 37,   HOW TO IDENTIFY YOUR GIFT   Note that we have done
some of Step 1 already.

EXERCISES TO BE DONE BEFORE CLASS--FILL OUT THE FOLLOWING QUESTIONNAIRES:

INWARD CONVICTION QUESTIONNAIRE

____ Do pages 102-104 which contain the "Inward Conviction
Questionnaire." Fill in as much as you possibly can.

____ Fill out page 105, HOW TO USE THE INWARD CONVICTION
QUESTIONNAIRE.

EXPERIENCE QUESTIONNAIRE

____ Do pages 113-120 which contain the "Experience Questionnaire"
and instructions for using it.

GIFTS CORRELATED TO TRAITS QUESTIONNAIRE

____ Do pages 98-101, the "Gifts Correlated To Traits Table."

SUMMARY OF FINDINGS--TO BE COMPLETED AFTER DOING QUESTIONNAIRES

instructions   Write down your findings thus far concerning your gift(s).

Exercise   Gift or Gifts Indicated

Inward Conviction Questionnaire

Experience Questionnaire

Gifts Correlated to Traits Questionnaire

REVIEW OF DEFINITIONS OF GIFTS

____ For each of the gifts listed above, review the definitions.   See
the appropriate page in Section II.   As you read the definitions of these
gifts, read them with this question in mind.   "Is this my gift?   Do these
things I am reading fit me?"

LESSON 11 OTHERS VIEW OF MY GIFT(S)

introduction We are continuing to work on identifying your gift. In lesson 10 we were analyzing background information which would help identify your gift. In this lesson we will be asking people who know you and have participated with you in some church related small group activity to help identify your gift or gifts. It is important to have the confirmation from others in the Body of Christ concerning your spiritual gifts.

purpose Lesson 11 seeks to help you do STEP 3 of HOW TO IDENTIFY YOUR GIFT. (See page 37)

STEP 3. SEEK CONFIRMATION OF YOUR GIFT FROM OTHERS.

objectives Here is what you will have accomplished by the time you finish Lesson 11. You will have,

- listed one or more gifts that are suggested from the "Outside Confirmation Form."

- reviewed the definitions of all gifts indicated on the "Form for Outside Confirmation."

choice of assignments Where time is limited you can expect your group leader to select assignments from the list which follows. Where adequate time is available you should do all of the assignments.

ASSIGNMENT CHECK-OFF LIST FOR LESSON 11

instructions   Below are the possible assignments for lesson 11. Do the ones
                assigned by your group leader.

READING FROM SECTION II TO BE DONE PRIOR TO QUESTIONNAIRES

____ Read again page 37, HOW TO IDENTIFY YOUR GIFT. Note that we
have done some of Steps 1 and 2 already and are presently on the
detailed follow-up suggestions for Step 3. Note carefully who
are the kinds of people that you should ask to fill out your
"Form for Outside Confirmation."

EXERCISES TO BE DONE BEFORE CLASS

FORM FOR OUTSIDE CONFIRMATION--TO BE FILLED OUT AND BROUGHT TO CLASS

____ Choose someone who knows you well to fill out the "Form For
Outside Confirmation." Have them fill out the "Form For Outside
Confirmation" in your presence so that they can discuss why they
answer questions the way they do (see pages 107-111).

SUMMARY OF FINDINGS--TO BE COMPLETED AFTER FORM HAS BEEN FILLED IN

instructions   List the gift or gift(s) indicated on the "Form For Outside
                Confirmation Form" below under the appropriate category.

<u>Gifts</u> <u>Marked</u> <u>Certain</u>   <u>Gifts</u> <u>Marked</u> <u>Potential</u>

REVIEW OF DEFINITIONS OF GIFTS

____ For each of the gifts listed above review the definitions. See
the appropriate page in Section II. As you read the definitions
of these gifts read them with this question in mind. "Is this
my gift? Do these things I am reading fit me?" Come to class
prepared to share what you have learned from this experience.

LESSON 12 MY VIEW OF THE GIFTS OF OTHERS

introduction   You have studied a good deal about spiritual gifts. You have talked to others about them. You have had help in identifying your own spiritual gifts. Now it is time to apply what you have learned and see if you can recognize when spiritual gifts are being used by others.

purpose   Lesson 12 forces you to begin to recognize the concept of an interdependent body. You will seek to identify gifts in others. And as you do so, you will recognize the importance of the ministry of the Spirit to you through others.

objectives   By the time you finish Lesson 12, you will have

● listed one or more gifts that you have seen in each of the members of your Spiritual Gifts Study class,

● filled out the "Form For Outside Confirmation" for one other class member of your Spiritual Gifts Study class,

● have filled out an observation form on some small group activity involving Christians in which you will indicate what you have seen in terms of Spiritual Gifts concepts.

choice
of
assignments   Where time is limited you can expect your group leader to select assignments from the list which follows. Where adequate time is available you should do all of the assignments.

ASSIGNMENT CHECK-OFF LIST FOR LESSON 12

instructions Below are the possible assignments for lesson 12. Do the ones assigned by your group leader.

READING FROM LESSON 1 OF SECTION IV TO BE DONE PRIOR TO OTHER EXERCISES

____ Read again Lesson 1 pages 3,4 containing the article "Gifts Are For Sharing." You read this article at the beginning of your study on Spiritual Gifts. Now you are much further along. You should be able to recognize the gifts of the people in the story.

EXERCISES TO BE DONE BEFORE CLASS

FORM FOR OUTSIDE CONFIRMATION--TO BE FILLED OUT AND BROUGHT TO CLASS

____ Choose someone who has been in your Spiritual Gifts Study class. You fill out the "Form For Outside Confirmation" (page 109) on that person and come to class prepared to share what you have written.

FILL OUT THE "CLASS LIST--GIFTS INDICATED" FORM

____ Fill out the form on Lesson 12, page 3. This form is used to list every person in your class and indicate gifts you have seen in them. Bring this with you to class and be prepared to tell why you have listed the gifts you did for each person.

OBSERVATION REPORT OF A SMALL GROUP ACTIVITY

____ Visit a Bible class or small group fellowship other than the Spiritual Gifts class. Fill out the Observation Report given on Lesson 12, page 4 and bring it to class with you.

ALTERNATE EXERCISE

____ Use either the "Gifts Correlated To Traits" (pages 99-101), the "Inward Conviction Questionnaire" (pages 102-104), or the "Experience Questionnaire" (pages 114-120) and interview some well-known leader in your church. You ask the questions and record the answers. Talk over the results with the person so as to get a clear picture of his/her gifts and the usefulness of the questionnaire. Bring your results to class and be prepared to share them with the group.

CLASS LIST--GIFTS INDICATED FORM

instructions   List each of your class members below. Beside their name list
gifts which you feel are appropriate. Potential Gifts mean
gifts which are very likely. Certain Gifts are gifts which you
feel have been amply demonstrated in the class itself so that
you could identify it clearly. Bring this form to class with
you and be prepared to share with the class why you put the
answers you did.

Name   Potential Gift(s)   Certain Gift(s)

OBSERVATION REPORT ON SMALL GROUP ACTIVITY

instructions   Attend some Christian small group activity. Use the questions below to help you observe the group from the perspective of Spiritual Gifts. Fill in whatever answers you can. Bring them with you to class and be prepared to share with the class.

1. How many people were in the group? ____
2. Of the people present how many actually participated in the activity by sharing, praying, teaching, etc? ____
3. Read carefully pages 63,64 giving the definition of the gift of exhortation. Look at all three aspects of this gift. Try to list somebody's name who shared in the meeting using one or more of the aspects of this gift:

   a. capacity to urge people to action in terms of applying Scriptural truth:
   b. capacity to encourage people generally with Scriptural truth:
   c. capacity to comfort people by applying truth to their needs:

4. Read carefully pages 69,70 giving the definition of the gift of faith. Look at the symptoms for this gift. Are there any indications that someone in the meeting has this gift? List the person and the indications.

   person   indications

5. Read carefully pages 54-56 giving the definition of the gift of teaching. Are there any indications in the meeting of anyone using this gift?

   person   indications

6. Read carefully pages 52,53 giving the definition of the gift of prophecy. Note carefully the symptoms for this gift. Are there any indications in the meeting of this gift?

   person   indications

7. Check here any other gifts which you felt were displayed in the group:

____ word of knowledge   if so, what was it?
____ word of wisdom   if so, what was it?
____ tongues   interpreted? what was it?
____ discernment   if so, what was sensed?
____ giving   how indicated?
____ evangelism   how indicated?
____ healing   who healed? of what? how?
____ governments   how seen?
____ helps   one indication.
____ mercy   indicated how?
____ miracles   what?

SUMMARY OF UNIT 4

introduction In Unit 4, you have studied lessons 10, 11, and 12. These lessons have allowed you to put into practice what you have learned about spiritual gifts. You have tried to recognize spiritual gifts both in yourself and in others.

REVIEW OF
EXPERIENTIAL
LEARNING

In lessons 10, 11, and 12 we,

- used three different background questionnaires to help you explore your own gifts: Inward Conviction, Experience, and Gifts Related to Traits,

- formulated a list of one or more of your gifts suggested from the questionnaires,

- reviewed the definitions of any spiritual gifts suggested by the questionnaires,

- had some other Christian suggest what gifts you had by filling out the Form for Outside Confirmation,

- reviewed the definitions of any gifts that were suggested on the Outside Confirmation Form,

- used what you have learned about spiritual gifts to identify the gifts of others.

LOOKING
AHEAD

At this point in your study you should feel that spiritual gifts are important. You know that the Holy Spirit has given at least one gift to each believer. And you know something about what these gifts are, enough that you can make tentative estimates about the gifts of others. You recognize that the Holy Spirit will minister to you through others. Knowing this will increase your trust in the Holy Spirit's ministry to you through others. You will also increasingly feel freer to minister to others because you know God has gifted you. You will probably have at least tentatively identified your main gift and perhaps a secondary gift. At this point, you should be ready for the emphases of the last lesson.

In the final lesson you will do preliminary planning for developing and using your gift.

LESSON 13 PLANS TO DEVELOP AND USE MY GIFT

introduction   Perhaps you will remember a statement I made in the preface to this revised edition of Spiritual Gifts. Let me repeat it.

"I have come to the conclusion that THE BIBLE EMPHASIZES THAT BELIEVERS SHOULD USE THEIR GIFTS. Whether or not they can identify them or develop them is a secondary matter. The study of spiritual gifts can easily sidetrack people to become overly occupied with identification of gifts.... My stress at the local church level is on using one's gift rather than identifying and knowing precisely what it is. In the context of service gifts emerge. Identification of gifts is difficult, if not impossible, apart from significant service by the believer.... The important thing at the local church level is the functioning of the body. Precise knowledge of one's gift is not necessary (though very helpful) to proper functioning of the body."

purposes   Lesson 13 seeks to motivate you to use your gift. Gifts develop in the context of use in the body. Lesson 13 seeks also to force you to think about what you can do to develop your effectiveness in using your spiritual gift.

comment   While lesson 13 seeks to accomplish the two main purposes listed, you should know from reading the quote above that the most important thing for you at this point is participation in small groups of believers in various Christian activities. In that kind of context the Holy Spirit will point out your gift and the need for interdependent ministry with others. At this point, there will be some studying these lessons who have not identified as yet their spiritual gifts. There will be others who are fairly certain that they have identified their gift(s). For those who have identified their gift, this lesson is pertinent and will be helpful. For those who have not yet identified their gift(s), do not be frustrated but recognize that you can participate in Christian activities and obey the Lord as He speaks to you and you will be using your gift whether you know what it is or not. Later, after some small group experience you may wish to come back and rework this lesson.

objectives   At the conclusion of lesson 13 you will have

• read through the suggestions I gave for developing the gifts you have tentatively identified as yours,

• listed 3 things you plan to do to develop your gift,

• listed one or more ways you intend to use your gift in a small group context (or in a larger group context).

assignments   Be sure you discuss with your group leader which assignments you personally should do.

ASSIGNMENT CHECK-OFF LIST FOR LESSON 13

instructions   Below are the possible assignments for lesson 13. Do the ones
assigned by your group leader.

EXERCISES TO BE DONE BEFORE CLASS

REVIEW LESSONS 10, 11, 12 TO LIST YOUR GIFT(S)

___ Scan your notes from Lessons 10, 11, 12 for information
regarding your personal spiritual gift. List the potential
gifts that you may have.

READ PERTINENT PORTIONS FROM SECTION III

___ For any potential gifts that you have listed read the
appropriate HOW TO DEVELOP THE GIFT OF _____ given in SECTION
III of SPIRITUAL GIFTS. See page 125 for the table of contents
concerning the development of gifts. Note any ideas (underline
them) which you feel may be helpful for you.

TALK OVER WITH YOUR GROUP LEADER DEVELOPMENT PLANS

___ Some gifts may not have development suggestions. If this is the
case, you should discuss with your group leader (or other mature
Christian having the gift of wisdom) how you could develop that
gift. Jot down any suggestions you get from this conversation.

LIST SOME DEFINITE STEPS YOU PLAN TO DO TO DEVELOP YOUR GIFT

--- List one thing you plan to do over the next month to
specifically work on developing one of your spiritual gifts.
This would be "one of the suggestions" which could be completed
in a month or less. Note your answer on the planning sheet,
lesson 13, page 3, and be prepared to share it with the class.

___ List one thing you plan to do over the next 3 months. This
would be a suggestion that would take longer to work on. Note
on the Planning Sheet lesson 13, page 3.

___ List a long range development suggestion. This would be a
suggestion which you plan to work toward during the next year or
two. Note this on the Planning Sheet on lesson 13, page 3.

LIST A SMALL GROUP ACTIVITY YOU PLAN TO PARTICIPATE IN

___ List here some small group activity you plan to engage in which
will help you use your gift. Tell how you think the activity
will help you use your gift.

PLANNING SHEET

instructions Note your suggestions for development and use of your gift.

ONE MONTH PLAN

I plan to do the following specific thing over the next month as a start
toward developing my spiritual gift:

THREE MONTH PLAN

I plan to do the following specific thing over the next 3 months as a start
toward developing my spiritual gift:

LONG RANGE PLANNING

I plan to do the following specific thing over the next year or two as a start
toward developing my spiritual gift:

personal   Sixteen years ago I did what I have asked you to do in this
note   lesson. God has helped me to continue to develop and use my
             gift. I am grateful that someone years ago helped me to plan on
             developing my spiritual gift. I hope you will feel the same way
             someday.

SMALL GROUP ACTIVITY TO USE MY GIFT

I plan to participate in the following small group activity in order to use my
spiritual gift and to be ministered to by others:

SUMMARY OF ALL UNITS

introduction   At this point you have completed your study on spiritual gifts.
                You will notice that we have followed the first 3 procedures of
                HOW TO IDENTIFY YOUR GIFT up to this point of the study. See
                page 37 for details.   Now we are to the fourth step of the
                procedure. It is up to you to do this in the years that follow.
                I include this step as a final word of exhortation from me.
                Read the step below, then ask the Lord to enable you to carry it
                out.

FINAL   Here is Step 4 of HOW TO IDENTIFY YOUR GIFT.
ASSIGNMENT

STEP PROCEDURE   EXPLANATION

4   SEEK TO LET   1. Your church will   increasingly be aware
      EXPERIENCE BE A   of gift(s) as you interdependently work
      DETERMINING FACTOR   in it.
      IN BRINGING OUT YOUR
      GIFT AS YOU MINISTER   2. You will be aware of fruit resulting from
      TO OTHERS.   the exercising of your gift interdependently
                                            with others.

                                         3. You will realize an increasing personal
                                            satisfaction in what you are doing.

                                         4. You will occasionally find that forced
                                            situations in your church will demand a
                                            needed gift which God may cause you to seek
                                            personally or to seek for someone in your
                                            group.

                                         5. You will recognize especially in the
                                            leadership gifts that gifted people will
                                            attract like-gifted people. Therefore, be
                                            ready to learn from those to whom you are
                                            drawn in ministry, often it will be because
                                            they have gifts like yourself. But be
                                            prepared also to help those who are drawn to
                                            your ministry. For they may be drawn to you
                                            because God has gifted them like you.

a final   I Peter 4:10, "As every person hath received the gift, even so
admonition   minister the same one to another, as good stewards of the
                manifold grace of God."

ADVICE TO THE GROUP LEADER

introduction   I assume that you, the group leader, have the gift of teaching and have developed it to the point where you are comfortable in small groups and can use discussion and sharing as a format in which you facilitate learning. For in studying <u>Spiritual Gifts</u> as a group you will be modelling the actual use of gifts in the group. You as a leader must see to it that people are motivated to do their assignments and learn how to share what they are learning with each other. People having exhortation gifts will be using them. People having wisdom or teaching will be using them. In fact many of the maturity growth gifts will be used in the context of sharing that will go on in the class. It is your job as a teacher/facilitator to see that the class develops as a community of gifted people sharing with each other. You should do every assignment that each of the members does. You should know the doctrine of spiritual gifts thoroughly. You should probably go through the booklet and Section IV doing all the assignments before the class ever begins. You should very early begin to recognize the symptoms of various gifts in people in the class. Your discussion questions and prompts should utilize this knowledge in who you ask what questions and how you encourage sharing. You must model the concept of trusting the Spirit's gifts in the people of the class. You will find this sort of class a great challenge. It is different from simply preparing a lesson and lecturing on it.

purposes   You should be always aware of the purposes of each lesson and
objectives   the objectives. Your questions and discussion prompts ought to be used to insure that objectives are being reached.

class format   The class should be primarily discussion. The discussion should center on clarification of what has been studied. It should also seek to motivate the class toward the identification and use of gifts. An atmosphere in which each is free to discuss, question, and exhort one another is a healthy structure in which gifts can emerge and be identified.

flow of   In general the flow of activities might include the following:
activities

> • Get-acquainted activities
> • Warm-up time
> • Discussion of previous assignments
> • Motivation toward the present assignment
> • Discussion of the present assignments and material
> • Clarification of assignments for the next lesson
> • Group Prayer

time   You will have to carefully watch the time. Discussion-type
schedule   classes can get away from the group leader so that very little
in a   gets accomplished. Be sure that Discussion of Previous
class   Assignments and Discussion of The Present Assignment gets the biggest portion of time.

ADVICE TO THE GROUP LEADER (cont.)

comment
on getting
acquainted

If the group already knows each other very well then you can
skip this activity. Otherwise, you must have this time, for
getting to know each other and becoming comfortable with each
other is essential to building community--the context in which
gifts emerge.

comment on
warm-up

Groups usually need just a bit of time at the beginning in which
they can get comfortable with each other again. I call this
warm-up time. You can do general sharing of what is going on in
lives, sing, whatever. Just recognize that most groups need a
transition from where they are when they arrive in the class to
the level of sharing you desire later on in the class.

comment on
previous
assignments

Often the lessons will have outside activities that are to be
done after the class. These experiential exercises form a very
important part of the total learning of the class. You should
always make sure that there is a period of time in the present
class to debrief, clarify, and discuss the outside learning
activities of the past week. This period of discussion will
often be the liveliest part of the class as people share their
experiential learning assignments. Encourage this sharing time.
Reflection on experiential learning changes values of people.

comment on
motivation

Try to motivate the class each time toward the importance of the
present lesson. You can use thought questions (see lesson 1 for
examples), or you can use illustrations from your past ministry
to challenge, or you can write simple case studies (see lesson
2, page 3 for a sample case study), or you can ask for the
class to suggest questions on things which were not clear to
them (you don't have to answer them at this time but get them
before the group to motivate them to listen and share later).
Sometimes you can ask a question like "What do you think God is
wanting to impress upon you in this lesson?" or "In what way do
you think the things we are learning in this present lesson are
needed in our church as a whole?" Each lesson requires special
motivation. You cannot assume that the class is motivated.

comment on
present
material
to be
learned

You should be thoroughly familiar with the material so that you
can answer most questions. Even though you may be able to
answer most questions, you should try to have the class members
answer questions as much as possible in order to allow their
gifts to emerge. You will most likely find that you will
disagree with some things I have written. Where that is so, you
should write your own definition, or comment, or biblical
example, etc. and pass them out to the class.

comment
on new
assignments

You should recognize that for some new assignments you will be
responsible to help the class members find people to interview
in outside activities. You should study the assignments well in
advance to identify those kind of responsibilities. See the
Table on the next page for help on this.

TABLE OF LESSON ITEMS TO BE PREPARED FOR BY GROUP LEADER

introduction   Many of the experiential learning activities will require people
to be interviewed. As group leader you should have lists of
names available to help the class members find someone to talk
to. Hopefully, the class members will be able to find someone
on their own but you should be prepared also to advise. This
may mean some advance contact work for you.

LESSON	ASSIGNMENT	EXPLANATION
1	GIFTS INTERVIEW SHEET	A list of full-time Christian workers who are willing to be interviewed concerning their knowledge and view of spiritual gifts. If your church has only a few, you may need to go outside your church to other churches and Christian organizations in your area.
1	GIFTS IDENTIFICATION SHEET	A list of mature Christians who will be interviewed concerning their understanding of spiritual gifts and recognition of same in their own church.
2	PROBLEMS INTERVIEW SHEET	A list of mature Christians who are aware of problems associated with spiritual gifts.
3	UNIQUE GIFTS IN I CORINTHIANS INTERVIEW SHEET	Two lists of Christians: List 1 of those who do not believe the supernatural gifts of I Corinthians exist for our day. List 2 of those who not only believe but practice some of these gifts in their church today.
4	UNIQUE GIFTS IN ROMANS	A list of mature Christians.
5	LEADERSHIP INTERVIEW	Two lists: List 1 of full-time Christian workers to be interviewed concerning their view of leadership gifts as seen in Ephesians 4 and List 2 of non-full-time Christian workers who exercise leadership in a church or organization.
7	MATURITY GIFTS CONVERSATION	A list of Christians who have one or more maturity growth gifts.
8	NUMERICAL GIFTS CONVERSATION	A list of Christians who have one or more numerical growth gifts.
9	ORGANIC GIFTS CONVERSATION	A list of Christians who have one or more organic growth gifts.

imitation   It would be very helpful if you would do all these outside
model   exercises yourself along with the class.

DETAILED LISTING OF TABLE OF CONTENTS

DETAILED LISTING OF TABLE OF CONTENTS (cont.)

ALPHABETIC LISTING OF GIFTS--DEFINITIONS

LISTING OF MAJOR MAPS OTHER THAN DEFINITIONS

LISTING OF HOW TO DEVELOP VARIOUS GIFTS

LISTING OF QUESTIONNAIRES AND OTHER FORMS

ORDER FORM

Name _____

Street Address _____

Mailing Address _____

_____

Phone _____

☐ Enclosed please find $11.95 for one copy of *Spiritual Gifts* ($9.95 plus $2.00 for shipping and handling).

☐ Enclosed please find $206.04 for one case (24 copies) of *Spiritual Gifts*, shrink–wrapped in packs of 6, ($9.95 per copy, less 40% discount, plus $15.00 shipping and handling).

Clip and mail this coupon to:

Horizon House Publishers
Drawer AA
Cathedral City, CA 92234
(619) 325–1770
Payable in U.S. funds